ADVANCE PRAISE FOR THE IMPACT OF SILENCE
GIVING YOURSELF PERMISSION

If you feel that you have spent too long living by the 'be seen and not heard' rule, Stephanie McAuliffe gives you the tools to be able to find and use your voice. Stephanie shares her powerful stories of how staying silent has impacted on her life physically, emotionally and spiritually. It is a wake-up call to give yourself permission to reclaim your sovereignty and move forward with joy.

I recommend this book to anyone who feels that they have been stopped from speaking-up in the past and now they are ready to connect to who they really are and let their light shine!

~Pat Duckworth, Women's Wellness &
Menopause Workplace Strategist

This book is so real and genuine. Stephanie shines this guiding light on the way our silence has shaped us. How we still by not speaking our truth allow it to shape our daily lives. It's truly awakening.

~ Melanie Robinson

"The Impact of Silence" invites us on a gentle but powerful journey to the truth of ourselves. Stephanie beautifully weaves together history, philosophy, and her own personal story to create a path to absolution, validation, and—ultimately—self-acceptance and the peace that comes with it. Warm without being cloying, sincere without being trite, Stephanie has created something few can claim—a practical map that anyone can follow that heals the mind and spirit.

~ Jennifer Kirby, Financial Advisor

Stephanie's ability to share her story with complete and utter vulnerability is absolutely amazing and powerful. Not only is her story impactful, but this book is a deep dive in so many amazing, beautiful layers of trust, intuition, and healing. It empowers the readers to remind them that they have the power within and to trust that the journey they are on is a personal one. I love Stephanie's ability to share her amazing tools and meditations especially my personal favorite, "joy." Highly recommended!

~ Robin Joy Meyers, Joy Architect,
Molecular Geneticist, Speaker, Author

THE IMPACT OF SILENCE

RECLAIM THE SOVEREIGNTY OF YOUR SOUL

STEPHANIE B. MCAULIFFE

FOREWORD BY
TRICIA BROUK

ISBN: 979-8-89079-247-1 (hardcover)
ISBN: 979-8-89079-282-2 (paperback)
ISBN: 979-8-89079-248-8 (ebook)

Legal disclaimer: This book is not to be used as a substitute for work with a mental health professional. The processes shared in this book are distinct from counseling, psychotherapy, or psychoanalysis and do not deal with the diagnosis or treatment of emotional or medical problems. Any and all actions resulting from reading this book are the responsibility of the reader as the sovereign and sole decision-maker for your life.

About the Author photo by Sierra Hinkley Photography
Cover photo by Candice McWhorter Creative

CONTENTS

Out of the depths rises the phoenix.

Out of the mud rises the lotus.

From the darkness emerges the light.

From the nest comes the bird.

Flying free.

Soaring.

With the past behind her in her trails. ~ SBM

This book is for the seekers in the world.

Take back your power.

Learn powerful tools and techniques to turn off the noise of the outside world.

SCAN ME

Go to:
wayofthediamondwarrior.com/PYE

FOREWORD

I met Stephanie at a networking cocktail party in New York City, one of those pre-winter, sideways-rainy kind of nights where not going is heavily considered because getting a cab is nearly impossible, and it's so much nicer to stay home warm and cozy. I was called to go. Back in 2017, I was not conscious of being called, so in my mind, I just decided to rally. I weathered the storm and walked into a room where I knew no one. Until I knew someone. Stephanie came right up to me, and with a powerful and confident voice, within moments, she invited herself to be a guest on my podcast, "The Big Talk." I remember the season was about what not to do before taking the stage, and she was willing to share all the mistakes she had made, including having a glass of wine right before going on and how that wasn't the smartest decision.

In this one conversation, amidst a sea of people who were all yelling over the loud music trying to be heard, we connected in a deep and meaningful way that led Stephanie to take my stage at the inaugural Speaker Salon at The Triad Theater. On day one, she walked onto the stage, and in total stillness and with absolute gravitas, she shared the story of how the sound of ice clinking in the glasses of her parents' cocktails haunted her. She shared how living with an alcoholic silenced her, and that healing from this codependence not only gave her voice, but it also gave her the power to teach others to use theirs.

I met Stephanie after she left Wall Street, which means I only know the spiritually awakened teacher she is today. Before each call in our Mastermind, she always tuned in so she would be in a state of receivership and able to fully support the other members. I know her to fire doctors based on her intuition. I know her to feel into her decisions when she's about to choose a new home. I know her to paint and write poetry and swing crystals. The calm, grounded, confident woman that is Stephanie always had a voice, and when she is silent by her choice, it was the kind washes over you with love and acceptance.

In *The Impact of Silence*, Stephanie uses her voice in truth and authenticity, dropping a few F-Bombs along the way while poetically reminding us we are not alone through her beautifully designed exercises and invitations.

She shows us what it looks like when our voices are silenced and how to tell if we are unconsciously silencing anyone else's voice. She reminds us of the power of energy and how it impacts us from the moment the egg is fertilized in Utero. This book's teachings are based not only on science but also the countless interviews she did with people who shared their personal stories of being silenced and how that infiltrated and permeated their work life, their personal life, and their identity.

She will teach you how to uncover and organically align with your truths, so you don't have to go to battle with your ego. She vulnerably shares her story, so you can learn from her healing and begin yours. The clearing of energy and practice of forgiveness that Stephanie covers can be difficult to grasp, yet she guides you through this process easily and impactfully. You will finally be able to release unhealthy relationships while birthing a new one with yourself. If you are called, like I was on that rainy night, Stephanie will help you free your voice, allowing you to move into the powerful being who is meant to be heard in the world. Read *The Impact of Silence*, knowing you are held.

Tricia Brouk
International Award-Winning
Director, Founder of The Big Talk Academy

INTRODUCTION
WE'RE AT A CROSSROADS

We're at a crossroads in human history, and the division feels wider than ever. I wrote the first edition of this book during a global pandemic. Since then, the challenges we're experiencing have only deepened.

We've been separated, and not just physically. Our underlying beliefs of who and how we are in the world continue to challenge the truth of who we are and where we fit in. Those in power want more control. Those who feel disempowered fight back. Our true colors are showing.

It's noisy. It's not pretty. Real change rarely is.

I've stood at my own crossroads. I found comfort in what was known even when I was uncomfortable with the current situation. Every time, I eventually listened to the wisdom in the silence and moved through what was calling me forth.

What emerged are levels of healing I didn't know were possible. I came to realize how much of my power I'd given away by allowing myself to be pulled into the undertow of my old stories—patterns I played on repeat, for myself and others.

Like me, you have a choice of how to move through the world. You can play into old fears, or connect with your inner voice in a different way, a voice that's true to you and one that only you can hear.

RIDE THE WAVE

In this book, I show you how to powerfully use silence and space to ease the burdens of the past. I also show you how to use this wisdom to live life from a new perspective.

Early on, we learned to be in the cycle of mindset – action – mindset – action – mindset – action, like riding a wave. We react when something comes up, which sets off the mind and spurs us to take action.

But our ego makes decisions based on what it knows.

Life will never be the same again. Change is the only constant. Even if you hope life will stand still, that never truly happens. True power lies in riding the wave and seeing your life from a new vantagepoint.

When you shift the underlying energy, you shift your mindset and come at life from a different space for different action.

The healing in your life can be as profound as you allow. The world says you can't change the past, but change is absolutely in your power. Begin by saying yes to yourself and understanding where the noise is coming from.

There is no story that can't be healed.

WHAT THE SPACE REVEALED

My ten-year marriage to a man I still loved and my twenty-seven-year career on Wall Street both ended within a year. I sat on my couch and didn't have a clue what to do next. The only things moving me forward were the need to eat, bathe, and occasionally see friends. I was shell-shocked by the sudden void in my life.

I now realize I experienced a mini nervous breakdown and PTSD. All of the emotions I'd pushed aside for so many years began to reveal themselves. I had nothing but myself to focus on, and that terrified me.

This was deeper than discontent, and I couldn't fix things myself. In my frustration, I sought out a therapist. I also attended Al-Anon meetings, a twelve-step group for those affected by someone else's alcoholism. Both brought me to a certain point but no further. That's when I had an epiphany. I was repeating my own stories in therapy and heard others repeating theirs in group meetings.

Through my initial work, I healed the damage from my two marriages to two alcoholics, which I share in my first book, *The Message in the Bottle: Finding Hope and Peace Amidst the Chaos of Living with an Alcoholic.*

I realized why so many people like me feel stuck. That opened the road for me to seek more.

THE ALCHEMY OF HEALING

The journey of this book is what came next, sharing portions of my own stories as well as those from clients and dozens of interviewees (all whose names have been changed for their confidentiality). Each chapter explores the key components of reclaiming the sovereignty of your soul. Walk with me as we explore happiness, health, freedom, family, school, faith & spirituality, and social connections.

We explore the science behind generational appropriation and why you feel the way you do, including processes to help you dissolve what's in your way.

While your experiences may be quite different, the impact of generational trauma and the silencing of who you are might have greater impact than you realize.

The Impact of a Noisy World

The world is filled with noise. It impacts us at every level of our being, including the stories we tell ourselves and the stories told to us. Seeking to quiet the noise and find peace, we swing the pendulum in the opposite direction, not knowing that we are shutting down more than the noise.

We silence the truth of who we are. We silence our individuality. Our brilliant ideas become dulled by the fear of being different, of standing out. One voice and one person at a time, each of us becomes a little dimmer, sometimes to the point of invisibility.

Life isn't meant to be lived this way. You have a purpose for being on the planet. Your life is as important and valid as everyone else's, even if you don't always feel this way.

Feeling silenced impacts every aspect of your life. When you feel stifled, you lose the joy and happiness of your experiences. When who you are isn't outwardly expressed, your challenges go inward and affect the physical, mental, emotional, and spiritual aspects of your life. This plays into your relationships—at home, at school, at work, and your social connections.

Awareness is the First Step Back to Freedom

Communication isn't solely via our spoken words. Most people I talk to—both clients and interviewees—express their desire for open and honest conversations without feeling defensive or judged.

We're supposed to know how to create boundaries, but few of us saw any real examples of this growing up. We grew up with rules.

We weren't taught how to express ourselves, nor were we taught to listen. This adds to the noise. As a result, we have little bandwidth for each other.

We want connection but don't know how to get there. Connection feels challenging, so instead, we distract ourselves from the pain of loss and feeling separate. We say "Fuck it!"

This is a global story we experience individually.

We each think our story is different, yet it often comes down to the same underlying theme. We're conditioned to give away our inherent power and put our life in the hands of others.

Awareness of these cycles is key to breaking out.

Is There a Conspiracy to Keep You Silent?

Being silenced isn't just about your words, but how you silence yourself and dull your light.

You might feel like the world and your mind have always conspired to silence your connection to yourself since before you can remember.

That might sound a little crazy.

Especially if you feel powerful and in control, as I did during my twenty-seven-year career on Wall Street.

Doing What We're Supposed to Do

My weekdays began with a 4:20 a.m. alarm. I was out the door by 5:30 in order to catch a boat into New York City. I'd be at my desk by 7:00. Many days, I'd arrive home between 7:00 and 8:00 p.m. My days were segmented into different levels of stress. I'd spend my evenings having dinner and a glass or two of wine, and be in bed by 10:00 p.m.

Your days may not be as hectic, but you still face obligations.

People who knew me back then saw a person who had a tight reign over what I did and how I moved through the world. I was on a mission to take on bigger and more challenging positions and projects.

I poured so much of myself into my work that I had little time or space for me. I didn't let myself into my own life. Proving myself meant perfection in my projects, so I wouldn't allow my own words or reactions to surface.

As I rose higher, I experienced a deeper disconnection to who I am. Less of me felt safe to share, especially as my marriage fell apart. I went into my own black hole, the same hole I dreamt about falling into when I was six, a story I share later in the book.

I did what I thought I was supposed to do. I buried what I shouldn't feel. I was a master of distraction.

This way of thinking and being came from prior generations. We're gaslit into feeling happy with what we have. We learn to base our worth on how we're seen by others.

Like almost everyone, I was gaslit, too. If you're like me, it's not your fault.

WE'RE FIGHTING AN OLD BATTLE

In *The Art of War*, written over 2,000 years ago, Sun Tzu speaks about the strategies of maneuvering around the enemy. "Let your plans be dark and impenetrable as night, and when you move, fall like a thunderbolt. He will conquer who has learnt the artifice of deviation."

War strategy goes as far back as we can remember, documented in petroglyphs and hieroglyphics that show epic battles won and lost. Leaders in battle learn strategy and deception to create an advantage over the enemy, even when they feel vulnerable.

When prior generations fought, persevered, and won, they had little bandwidth for personal problems. They learned to suck it up, just like we did.

WHAT'S REAL?

You're surrounded by messages from family, friends, church, society, politicians, marketers, TV, and the news. They yammer in your ear all day long and tell you what they think you want to hear, or why you're not good enough, or why you like or dislike something. They want you to come over to their way of thinking, doing, being, or buying.

Messages to distrust who you are run deep. Belly fat, cellulite, wrinkles, hair color, what you eat, how you eat, when you eat, why you eat—they're never right in someone's mind or their marketing message. The same for how you dress, how you live, where you live, and the car you drive.

Doubt will make you shrink in ways you may not realize. When you feel you don't measure up, you tend to hide or stay small.

If you could find sanctuary by driving an SUV, as marketed in ads for the Lincoln Navigator, the world would be a peaceful place. While a $65,000 vehicle may feel nice to drive, the comfort is temporary and doesn't create real long-lasting peace. This is just one example of how marketing messages tell you that something outside of you will wipe your troubles away.

USING YOUR INTUITION

Plato's *Republic* defines intuition as a "fundamental capacity of human reason to comprehend the true nature of reality."

When you connect with your intuition and wisdom, you begin to turn off the noise of the outside world.

You begin to hear the whispers of who you are. These whispers are your higher self and soul talking to you. Your soul is on a journey with you as a catalyst in this lifetime. Through growth you evolve, and your soul only wants the best for you.

Think of your higher self as your extension of you.

∞ It's the greatest aspect of you.

∞ It's the part of you that hasn't been wounded.

∞ It's not connected to your stories.

∞ It's you at your purest level.

This is your access to higher wisdom, consciousness, and God. You are a divine child of God.

DISCOMFORT WITH GOD

For many years, I was afraid of saying the word God. When people used the term, my insides winced. I declared myself an atheist in my teens and went for decades without any spirituality. I filled the void inside me by proving myself in the world.

The word God makes many people feel uncomfortable. It carries a lot of baggage. Rightly so.

In this book, I refer to God in two ways:

- ∞ In my formative years, the God I refer to is of the Episcopal Church where I was raised.
- ∞ In recent years, I might refer to God as Spirit, Consciousness, Christ Consciousness, and the Universe.

God is much bigger than a man in a white robe sitting in judgment from up on a cloud.

The God I speak of now knows only love. Love isn't logical. It shines.

HOW TO USE THIS BOOK AND WHAT TO EXPECT

In this book, I share many of the ways we have been silenced, success stories from my work with clients, insights from interviews, and portions of my journey.

I share key components from what I've learned: how twenty-seven years on Wall Street was the perfect foil, the importance of energy healing work, and what it means to come back to yourself.

When you connect with the truth of who you are, your individuality, and your creativity as a human being, you shine. Your belief systems shift. You experience the world from a new perspective, and you're less triggered by the past.

You act rather than react.

- ∞ By making a conscious choice to turn off the noise of the outside world, you can reclaim the parts of yourself you have lost along the way. You become more trusting of yourself and your intuition. When the world around you disagrees, you can stand firmly in what's right for you.

You understand why you feel the way you do, so you can be free of judgment, whether from yourself or others.

∞ By speaking your truth from love, you create a different level of connection in your relationships, where you don't feel like you're walking on eggshells. You see people and love them for who they are: unique and on their own journey.

Your soul asks this of you because it, too, wants to connect.

No matter where you are on your path, you will continue to learn about your human existence with a deeper richness and joy.

You will wear the world around you like a loose garment, untethered from the stories that used to define you. That's powerful AF.

Living in the freedom of who you are has never felt more important. You have tremendous abundance to experience beyond the noise of the world.

Let's begin this journey together.

~Stephanie B. McAuliffe
December 2024

CHAPTER 1
WHY LIFE FEELS LIKE A SILENT, INVISIBLE BATTLE

"When awareness is brought to an emotion,
power is brought to your life."
~ Tara Meyer Robson

When life feels like you're fighting an invisible battle, you don't know what's safe to share and how to express yourself.

You feel like you're standing on a rocky shore in a storm. Like the world is knocking you around, and you don't know where the wind is coming from.

How did you get to this place of not feeling safe to speak, of systemically silencing yourself to the point where your insides are screaming? How did you get into this mess?

THE INSANITY OF LIVING A LOGICAL LIFE

When I was young, I loved math, especially geometry proofs. I found satisfaction in solving complex puzzles and figuring out how the pieces fit together. Logic gave me something concrete to sink my teeth into, and the results were tangible.

When I was graduating from high school and floundering to find my direction, my father gave me a meeting with a management consultant as a graduation gift. The aptitude test pointed to two key careers: computers and art.

I loved art and the flow of the creative mind. I savored my time in art classes. But at the age of sixteen, I fed into the idea of the starving artist. I didn't want to experience that, so I chose computers.

As a computer programmer, I got to blend my love of both art and logic. This continued as I moved up the corporate ladder, first into project management and then into managing large corporate programs.

Logic meant I didn't have to pay attention to what was going on inside of me.

---

*Logic meant I didn't have to pay attention
to what was going on inside of me.*

How do logic and data provide a certain sense of comfort?

We live in a logical society, more so since the advent of the Industrial Revolution. We want data and evidence for what we see and experience. Data and evidence are incredible partners for the advancement of technology, science, and medicine. But when we fully rely on logic and brainpower to move us through life, we disconnect from our heart and our intuition.

Logic becomes really noisy when you use your brain to make an emotional decision. Sometimes, you can feel like you're beating your head against the wall. When you can't find a logical answer, what you hear and see outside of you plays on your internal doubt.

THE CYCLE OF DOUBT AND SILENCE

When was the last time you saw an ad that told you, "You have everything you need! You're perfect as you are. Keep doing you." These messages are few and far between. Businesses and marketers make money on your need to feel better, be better, and to be more of something. They play off of your doubts and fears, rather than your perfections.

Doubt is their weapon, so you'll need their product.

Doubt breeds silence because you feel safer hiding your questions about yourself or a situation. With silence you become attached to your trauma. This turns into a vicious cycle because when you can't speak about something, you numb to it.

Sometimes, silence stems from your trauma. In that case, speaking means becoming retraumatized and wondering what you did wrong.

This pits you against your own emotions in order to feel some modicum of control.

THE IMPACT SINCE THE INDUSTRIAL REVOLUTION

Even two or three generations ago, few people had consideration for mental health. The Industrial Revolution left little room for more than existing through the day-to-day. We had less space for our emotions.

Each generation felt the impact of the battles they fought, and each was silenced as part of their societal experience.

Those who went through WWI were known as The Lost Generation. They fought for freedom, but when they returned, they didn't feel safe to speak about the atrocities they'd seen. The phrase *shell shocked* originated in WWI, a term used to describe the PTSD many soldiers experienced during the war.

The Silent Generation experienced the Great Depression when people fought for survival. They had little space for feelings. During this time, many believed they were seeing the end of the American dream.

The phrase "suck it up" originated from WWII pilots, when they had to suck it up if they vomited into their oxygen masks. Otherwise, they risked suffocating or choking. Unfortunately, this phrase now extends into the broader spectrum of life.

Early Baby Boomers experienced McCarthyism where fear was a weapon of repression and persecution for those who spoke up in favor of "left wing" ideas.

Baby Boomers also fought in Vietnam and experienced the shunning of society similar to those who fought WWI.

Gen X grew up with the societal impacts of Vietnam. This forgotten generation saw both parents enter the workforce, hence the term latch-key kids.

Millennials are a generation that's more civic minded, yet many of them were raised by Baby Boomers who continued the rules of silence from their youth, i.e., don't speak unless you're spoken to.

Gen Z is now called The New Silent Generation. This generation has better awareness and diagnosis of mental health conditions. However, they're also diagnosed at higher levels than their predecessors.

For generations, we've been conditioned to suppress and silence who we are, what we think, and how we feel. This learned behavior is compounded, with each generation creating patterns of silencing our words and our wounds.

When you grow up with the generational pattern of silencing your emotions, you have little space to express yourself.

WHEN THE OPPRESSED BECOMES THE OPPRESSOR

Sometimes, the quest for survival cuts off the very people who were with you in battle, which creates newer and deeper wounds. Not all wounds are intentional, yet society creates a ripple effect through whole swaths of a generation.

For women, coming into your own is a repeated pattern of trying to fight your way "in," so your voice can be heard. I saw this repeatedly while on Wall Street. Unfortunately, sometimes women are the least supportive of each other.

The struggle continues over a woman's right to be seen and heard. We could go down the rabbit hole of women's rights, but that isn't the purpose of this book.

When a suppressed group finds their voice and starts feeling heard, they sometimes suppress a subset of voices within the group for fear that their message might become diluted.

This has been documented in the women's suffrage movement, where Northern white women excluded the voices of black women and partnered with Southern white women out of their fear of losing their place. In her book, *The Suffragettes Were Not Allies to Black Women, They Were Racist*, ShaRhonda Knott-Dawson stated, "That the inclusion of White women in democracy was more important than any racial inclusiveness at all." All because black men were given the right to vote before white women.

People you thought you could trust might suddenly shift. At that point, you have no recourse because the battle you thought you were fighting has changed. This is a strategy of divide and conquer. White women became focused on their own inclusion, on not staying silenced. Black women were suddenly left on the sidelines, by both black men and white women. They were silenced in a whole new way.

WHO'S REALLY WINNING?

With the suppression of emotions, old ideals continue to play out as you try to protect your space. Most people haven't evolved beyond the silencing and quashing of ourselves across generations, nor across genders or races.

People and organizations that want control still play on your fear of not fitting in. Social media intensifies this because people feel they have the right to call each other out.

Social media has given a voice to millions, but what they express isn't always healthy. Social media provides a forum for people to project their wounds toward anything that triggers them, rather than taking responsibility for their feelings. No one wins if our empowerment disempowers someone else.

No one wins if our empowerment disempowers someone else.

However, we can't blame where we are on social media. It's just another forum.

For many generations, messages have been coming at us. Social media has amplified the number of those messages on a moment-by-moment basis. If you're not on Facebook, Instagram, or X, a marketing ad on the side of a bus or train is still social media. Marketing messages have been in print newspapers for centuries.

They tell you that the way you live your life is wrong.

- ∞ You need this to fulfill you.
- ∞ This is what you really want.
- ∞ You need to be....
- ∞ Do this and think this way because we know better than you.

This constant barrage of questioning your very being is a continuation of what began when you were young.

QUESTIONING YOUR PARENTS

When Sarah was in second grade, she had fainting spells and ended up in the hospital. Rather than asking her for more information, her parents *told* her why she was there—she wanted attention. They never asked her if she needed help. They never asked her what was going on with her to make this happen in the first place.

She thought her parents telling her why she fainted was normal because children don't question their parents. They didn't want to hear about her feelings, so she suppressed them.

As an African-American woman who grew up in the South, the generations before her were conditioned to not ask. Questions created trouble. Questions could be dangerous. What Sarah experienced was an extension of how her family found safety in silence.

If you grew up in a family with tension, trauma, addiction, mental illness, or stress, this might have added to the silencing. Not only did the family avoid talking about what was happening, as a child you may have felt unsafe to speak up. You found ways to manage despite what you saw in your environment.

How Big is Your Puddle?

Think of a puppy who peed on the floor. She tried to hold it in, and you can see by the look in her eyes that she knows she made a mess. The reaction to the puddle can be one of shaming, or it can be one of creating an environment to learn, clean things up, and move forward.

If the response in your household was to pour on guilt or shame, or you were ignored, the natural reaction is to bury your experience. This creates an internalized story of why your discomfort wasn't supported, and that story carries forward into adulthood.

You may be less apt to try new things because creativity and expansion involve something new. The anticipation of stepping into your own puddle may stop you from trying in the first place.

What Truth Are You Telling?

Have you ever told someone what you think they want to hear, rather than being straight up about what's really happening and how you feel?

Did you act that way out of fear of their response and the repercussions?

Telling people what you think they want to hear is one impact of silence. It silences you and robs the other person of expressing themselves in return. It silences the opportunity for a positive exchange that goes beyond words.

Telling people what you think they want to hear is one impact of silence.

WE'VE BEEN SCHOOLED

Through rules and the attempt to create efficiency, we've lost the connection to our creativity. In school, during after-school activities and sports, along with our to-do list on the path to success, our younger days were regimented.

Teachers force kids into compliance to make things easier in the classroom. Adults try to get kids to be who they want them to be, rather than who they truly are.

School is a rehearsal for life. When you're forced to conform, you can't fully connect with your gifts or talents. When they have a procedure for how to ask questions, the education system stifles curiosity and creativity.

When you give crayons and a blank piece of paper to a four-year-old, they rarely say, I don't know what to do with this. That's not always true for an adult. At some point, you realize that you might get it wrong, so you silence yourself and stay safe.

As a child, you didn't know how to ask for what you wanted. You had little leeway for exploration. With that in mind, there's a good reason why you, as an adult, may have difficulty making decisions.

WE WERE TAUGHT TO NOT SPEAK UP

Laura, an interviewee, said, "I was taught from an early age that there would be tremendous punishment at the back end for speaking up. Mostly emotional from my dad, it was punishment from others, and a lot of betrayal. Mostly just rejection and punishment."

She continued, "The impact of being silenced on me was so profound. The way I learned to survive was to not fight, to not play. I froze. I waited it out."

When you're in a state of fear, you can't access your own answers or truly hear yourself.

If you grew up in a perpetual state of survival, you never really had a chance.

How could you thrive?

Laura continues, "It's not terrifying with my husband anymore, but it used to be. It took years for me to have enough experience with him to know that it wouldn't end things, or I wouldn't be ostracized."

For you, not getting immediate insight or having a quick response can feel like you're in a dark room and can't find the light. As an adult, your subconscious may still be waiting it out. You may find yourself with your boss, your partner, or your kids, struggling to articulate your point of view when they may not agree with you.

SPIRITUAL CONFUSION

Spiritual movements have done their own damage in silencing us.

∞ Just look forward.

∞ Don't worry, be happy.

∞ All things love and light.

Looking at only the positive side of things comes with great danger.

Within us we all have some darkness, also referred to as our shadow. Mistakes are part of the human experience. When leaders claim there is no dark energy and only light, they dismiss huge aspects of our past waiting to be healed.

There is absolutely love and light. There is also hate, fear, and darkness. To see one without the other leaves you with an incomplete lens. This is called spiritual bypassing of karma that's here to be cleared.

Yes, dwelling on the negative may take you down a rabbit hole, and you might be challenged to climb out of it. But when you only look at the bright side, the rabbit hole keeps getting deeper. When you finally fall in, you have to deal with all the shit you've ignored.

When you only look at the bright side,
the rabbit hole keeps getting deeper.

Ever wonder why spirituality can feel so confusing?

PRETENDING IN BLISS

When you look the other way, you can pretend you didn't see what you just saw. When you pretend you don't hear something, you can claim ignorance. Yet, every act and every whisper has associated energy—in the office, at home, at church, and in social gatherings.

Sometimes looking the other way is a good thing. A drunk person fondling themselves on the New York City subway is something you would like to un-see.

Closing your ears to an argument may keep you from absorbing the energy of their exchange, but what if the energy of those words is familiar to you?

Perhaps by closing your ears, you miss an opportunity to look more deeply at a personal situation and clear something for yourself. Maybe you missed an opportunity to witness a healthy disagreement, especially if your formative years didn't include this kind of interaction.

You can pretend to bliss yourself out and be fully present in the now. Being fully present also means dealing with the shit sandwich that's sitting right in front of you. Ignoring it doesn't make it go away. When you no longer look at it, you may think you're done. But you've deceived yourself.

The energy of the shit sandwich remains with you, and you'll expend untold amounts of energy trying to ignore it. You'll need more and more bliss to maintain it when you could have used much less time and effort to resolve your shit in the first place.

HOW DO YOU USE YOUR VOICE?

Our collective communication is shut down, not only in the world around us but also within ourselves.

We use devices and technology to break the loneliness and fill the void. But that connection and communication aren't true representations of life. They rarely fulfill the longing to be seen and heard.

Society makes us feel that people who don't agree with us are the other. Some treat those others as the enemy. Deep separation puts us into camps that say, you're either with us or you're against us.

We can easily blame society. But society is made up of families that are made up of people, the same as companies and organizations.

How ironic that we appear to have many outlets to speak up, yet our voices come out as noise. When you express yourself, does your energy go toward fighting old battles, or does it create something different?

How ironic that we appear to have many outlets to speak up, yet our voices come out as noise.

ALBERT EINSTEIN WAS RIGHT

The results of that aptitude test took my career decision out of my hands. It was an either/or in a very small realm of possibilities. At the time, I found comfort in having someone (or a test result) tell me what I was good at because I had absolutely no idea how to choose for myself.

My path was chosen for me because I didn't know what my heart wanted. In a way, my heart spoke through that test. I used its answer to move through life. This would prove to be one of my biggest challenges when my Wall Street career ended.

No wonder that as an adult, I didn't know what the fuck I wanted or how to get it, because I rarely got any experience in that area.

What practice did you get? You may have had few choices, or maybe you weren't even included in the conversation.

If you weren't taught to express your wants or needs, if you didn't have a safe space to ponder your dreams, the pressure as an adult feels harder.

Albert Einstein said, "We can't solve problems by using the same kind of thinking we used when we created them."

What we experience in our day-to-day life has built up over centuries of conditioning. We fight the good fight. But who's fight is it really?

Life isn't logical. But that's the way we've been taught to live it.

Life isn't logical.

Your Invitation: Make a list of situations in your life where you've felt silenced and where you used logic over emotion. Look closely at your family. While this invitation may not feel comfortable, this awareness is a powerful step forward in your evolution.

Find paper, crayons or colored pencils and draw, without judgment. Don't think about what you want to draw. Allow an image to come to you intuitively. Imagine you are your younger self who has complete freedom. Have fun and play. Creativity, like life, isn't always logical.

CHAPTER 2
HOW YOUR AGENCY IS SILENCED

"There comes a time when silence is betrayal."
~ Martin Luther King Jr.

A NEFARIOUS CONSTRUCT

One of the phrases I remember from my formative years is, "Children should be seen and not heard." I heard it from my parents and my grandparents.

I remember the cocktail parties my mother and stepfather used to have. The kids were allowed to mingle now and then, but the general rule was to not speak unless you were spoken to. When I look back to these times, I felt invisible in a roomful of people. Not only was my voice silenced, but I felt odd in my own home. I was there, but was I really?

"Children should be seen and not heard" is a complicated phrase and one of the most nefarious constructs we live with. This saying was written by a clergyman and first documented in the mid-1450s. His writing was directed toward young women, saying they should not speak when around adults unless they were first addressed. Exactly when it took on the energy of applying this to children is unclear.

Religion adds to this premise in the Fourth Commandment in the Bible, "Honor thy father and mother."

This statement runs deep and has many layers. It tells our children they have no agency. They're just along for the ride. They hear: We're moving. We're giving away the dog. You're getting a little brother. You're getting a new father/mother.

Adult decisions must be made by an adult. However, when kids are brought into the conversation, they feel informed beforehand, rather than reacting after the fact and feeling like the rug was pulled out from under them.

PATRICIA'S STORY OF INVISIBILITY

Patricia was born with a heart condition and spent her first six months in the hospital. Her father left when she was four months old. He visited her periodically until the age of three when he moved West and contact ceased.

Her mother expressed how she felt abandoned but gave no acknowledgment that Patricia had also been abandoned. Patricia never knew her father—his personality, how he saw the world, or how he felt about his daughter. They had no discussion about him at all.

Growing up with heart disease and other difficult circumstances, she felt like Katelin in the movie, *The Titanic*, like she was screaming at the top of her lungs, but no one could hear. She had a sense that if something extreme happened, she would finally be seen and acknowledged. Instead, she carried into her adult life the feeling that she could be in a roomful of people and still be completely invisible.

When a child feels they don't have a voice, their parents are quietly saying, "I birthed you, so you're an accessory, and you're coming along for the ride." They feel silenced.

This fear of speaking up will silence every decibel that wants to come through your throat. The energy of your unexpressed words becomes internalized, buried deep within your cells.

NO NEED FOR EXPLANATIONS

Here is a deeper implication.

In many households:

- ∞ Children aren't seen as full humans until adulthood.
- ∞ Children don't know what's going on, so their parent's actions don't have a lasting effect.
- ∞ Parents feel no need for explanations.

We've learned otherwise. Younger generations are much more aware of how open and receptive children are.

Generations of people continue to live with the idea that children don't have a say, or the right to question, until they become adults.

Did you ever hear, "When you're on your own and paying your own rent, you can have a say?"

I've had many conversations with adults who believe their kids aren't aware. I had a friend whose wife was challenged with mental illness. He told me their six-year-old son didn't know what was happening to her.

In the logical adult brain, these parents wanted to think their child wasn't affected or aware of the energy in their environment, but their son was shut down. They deeply loved him and believed they were protecting him.

As a form of protection, silence has the exact opposite effect.

I've interviewed countless friends, colleagues, and clients who've shared stories of how they were not talked to, especially in the case of divorce. This dismissal pierces your heart, and the lack of closure weighs on you—like a death no one talks about.

Suddenly, home isn't the same, and your emotions have nowhere to go.

This robs you of the opportunity to learn how to have nourishing coping mechanisms.

WORDS CAST SPELLS

Words Cast Spells

Words, silent and spoken, create entire universes, especially for children.

CHILDHOOD IS NOT THAT OLD

The concept of childhood is relatively new. For centuries, children went to school until a young age, if at all. Afterward, they went to work on a farm or supported the family through other work. Wealthy classes were more privileged, yet they still had the rule that children only spoke when spoken to.

Children need a level of discipline as they grow. How to function within the family is learned though rules, and through rules they learn where the boundaries are.

When children are treated as property with strict lines as to when and how they will be seen and heard, the suppression affects more than their words.

In our society childhood is a norm, where both boys and girls go to school and choose a career, rather than the old paradigm where the girls marry to be supported by their spouse and have babies. Children usually fall in line with family and church dynamics. This still runs deep in some segments of society.

No one is immune, no matter how good things look from the outside. We continue to turn down our dial, sometimes to the point of being numb. However, being numb doesn't mean we're immune to the energy of events around us.

We know and feel far more than we acknowledge.

EVERYTHING IS GOING TO BE OK?

In my third year of life, my mother became pregnant with my youngest brother. During that time, she experienced deep depression and required three weeks of treatment away from home.

At three years old, I wasn't able to articulate my feelings. The adults raising me were experiencing a serious medical challenge. At that time, people didn't talk about mental illness, nor its broader effects. The adults in my family didn't understand the impact her mental illness had on me as a child. I also didn't comprehend what was happening.

The most important message I could have heard back then is that everything was going to be okay.

WHAT'S TRUE?

A unique cauldron exists in every house, an alchemy of the energy and emotions of each of the inhabitants. From the moment you enter, you bring to the cauldron all that is you.

You learned when to be quiet, when you are safe to speak, and when to get the hell out.

Early on, you may have questioned, *What did I do wrong? Why can't I say that?* Then the thoughts, *Is this safe? Can I say this?* You begin to temper your words. You begin to question what you see and what to say. *Am I seeing what I think I see? What's true here?*

In the movie, *Tommy*, the deaf, dumb, and blind boy witnesses an affair and murder. He was told, "You didn't see it. You didn't hear it. You won't say nothin' to no one ever in your life." This gaslighting is similar to what we experience in real life.

JUDGED BY GOD

The church I grew up in instilled from an early age that the world contains good and evil, and that I was born with sin. I was bad and flawed from the get-go, and I needed religion to be a better person.

When I was six, I dreamt I fell through a hole in my kitchen floor and began a free-fall into hell. I remember the terror and the feeling of being totally out of control. I was afraid I'd done something so wrong that God was punishing me, even though the old man down the street was the one who was improper. The fear of being judged by God instilled a good-girl perfectionism that ran through me for many years.

Religion has many good things, including community. But when the leader instills fear of punishment and promises rewards for subservience, is religion propping you up or pulling you down to control you?

When you're taught that asking questions is not safe, you've been subjugated. Your level of silence matches the amount of control over you.

---

*Your level of silence matches the
amount of control over you.*

Whether you attend a church, a mosque, a synagogue, or some other type of spiritual center, you'd like to think of them as safe places that support your true growth. Just like home.

You hear in the same presentation that you're both good and you've sinned, and more importantly, that if you sinned you can't be good. Your brain picks up on the negative messages, week after week, and you question yourself. You must repent for being human, and for being yourself. How does this in any way lift you up?

People have stepped away from organized religion for good reasons. Many of them walk through life without any spirituality, as I did for many years.

LIKE FLIES IN HONEY

As a child, you took on many things that were never yours in the first place. It's not your fault. You didn't know any better, and most of the time, you didn't realize what was happening to you, especially energetically.

Your thoughts as a child get stuck inside you like flies in honey.

---

*Your thoughts as a child get stuck
inside you like flies in honey.*

What you lacked in childhood will follow you into your adult relationships and how you present yourself in the world. Not feeling seen may continue as it did for Patricia, or it may show up many years later, as it did for me.

My career was the perfect foil to prove I was worthy. I put my health and wellbeing aside to receive the recognition I still craved. When I did receive acknowledgement, the satisfaction didn't last long because it came from the wrong source—external things I thought could fill my internal void.

The feeling of lack is rarely from only the recent generation before you. We carry a trail of learned behaviors that continue to affect the family dynamic and home environment for decades, even centuries. Sometimes, support from family can be incredibly positive. Other times not.

A DIABOLICAL BETRAYAL

When we're young, we don't think of our parents as humans. They're authority figures. Yet, they're facing their own challenges in life, and responding to their own fears and pain. When they were in the middle of their own challenges, they may have had little room for yours.

Feeling silenced prevents you from having hard and necessary conversations. You have an energetic wall around you. You can't see it, but you can certainly feel it. This is where you shift from saying the truth to softening your words or saying what you think someone wants to hear.

This feels like a diabolical betrayal of your integrity, which continues to dim your light.

LOSING GOD

When I was completing my freshman year of high school, my mother and stepfather divorced, and we moved to Florida. The move was a great relief as I left the house I'd shared with my stepbrother. By that time, I was old enough to stop the sexual abuse that had taken place for over four years.

In Florida, I blossomed. I no longer had to look over my shoulder or live with the everyday reminders. I began to come into myself as my nervous system was finally able to relax. It was an incredibly powerful time for me.

At Christmas of my junior year, my mother decided to remarry my stepfather. Before the beginning of the next school year, we would move back north.

My world crumbled out from underneath me. Again, I expressed myself in many ways, none of them healthy. I experimented with hard drugs. I slept with many boys. My grades went from As to Cs. I just didn't give a shit.

My favorite word became "whatever." I tried to brush away the hurt and betrayal, even though my heart felt deeply wounded.

The day I was to fly north, I sat on a bench outside the Sarasota airport and cried for hours, and finally pulled myself together for my flight. I don't remember a lot about my first few weeks in Massachusetts. I've been told I cried for two weeks. What I do remember hearing is, "Stop crying. You're driving me crazy."

We had no conversation, nor room for my emotions. No, "I know this is hard for you, but I felt like I had no other choice." No hugs. Although, I don't know if I would have accepted them, as I felt totally and completely abandoned and sacrificed. I rebelled.

Within two weeks, I found the kids who partied. I fell back into hard drugs. When my mother tried to ground me, I ran away. After some nights away, I returned on Thanksgiving Day.

I remember sitting at the table, my mother to my left, when I announced that I was an atheist. I no longer believed in God. I was completely and totally shut down, and making one last attempt to get her attention. I put a complete wall around my heart. Everything felt black and dark. I had nothing left.

IT'S NOT PERSONAL

Your parents were living their lives. Sometimes, you were an afterthought. This may feel like a brutal statement. It is. And it's true. It's nothing personal.

That doesn't mean they didn't care. Most do their best with what they have. This includes the emotional capacity to see beyond themselves.

Often, people don't understand the emotional impact they have on someone else. Even when you think you're doing the right thing, that doesn't mean it's right for the other person.

When you don't ask, you don't know.

When you don't ask, you don't know. This is an instance where silence can be more damaging than the act itself. Without conversation, your mind goes into overdrive. You're simply left to wonder.

WE'RE ALL HUMAN

Who raised you, and who raised them? When you look beyond your upbringing and beyond the secrets to their behavior, you find their hurtful actions were reactions to their pain, and not personal toward you.

This doesn't mean that what happened didn't sting. It means the people around you are human.

Barbara grew up feeling like her mother competed against her, which demonstrated a complete lack of boundaries. Barbara was also responsible to care for her siblings. Through our work together, she created healthier boundaries with her sister and created space for herself. She let go of old "obligations."

SEEING YOUR PARENT AS HUMAN

When you see your parent as a human being, the pedestal disappears, and you see the person who raised you in a different light. When that happens, you might feel some mourning.

Your mental image of what a parent should be and how you should have been raised may change. You might also feel deep seeded emotions, such as anger, disappointment, or sadness.

This isn't about judging the people who raised you. It's about coming full circle to see how their life impacted you and how their parents impacted them. Take this opportunity to see them with empathy and open the door for healing.

Their advanced age doesn't mean they have the same emotional capacity as you do. Stifling your emotions stunts the growth of a critical aspect of self. Through healing, your emotional age can catch up to your linear age.

THE SPIDERWEB INTO WHICH YOU'RE WOVEN

You can point a finger, but you have no place to point it. Where would you start?

BEING THE OBSERVER

Look more closely at your family of origin and the way you've interacted with them. Take a few moments to look at a specific situation from the perspective of the observer.

View it as if you're looking at a play from a balcony, where you're also one of the characters on the stage. Notice the energy of the situation and the interconnections. Each person has their own truth, and then there's the truth of the situation.

Your Invitation: Draw your family tree as far as you wish to go—you, your siblings, parents, grandparents, aunts & uncles, and cousins. Next to each person's name, write adjectives to describe them. When you see this on paper, you may begin to see a different perspective of the interplay and the threads of your spiderweb.

If you were to reflect on one scene in the play of your life, who are the actors? What's the storyline? Going a little deeper, what are the energetic ties between each person? You might see five people, each with their connections to the others, and all of you acting as catalysts for each other.

CHAPTER 3
THE SILENT ABSORPTION OF THE WORLD AROUND YOU

"Children are the living messages
we send to a time we will not see."
~ John F. Kennedy

THE ENERGETIC SIGNATURE YOU TAKE ON IN THE WOMB

You may think of your gestation as being silent, but even before you left the darkness and safety of the womb, you took on the energy and emotions of your birth mother. You felt everything she felt. You felt everything she thought. Her anxiety was your anxiety. Her sadness, your sadness. Her joy, your joy. All these emotions carry an energetic signature.

Some argue that a fetus can't feel. Until a certain point, this is true, and this isn't about pro-choice or pro-life. The energy of the sperm meeting the egg creates the fetus, and it develops via energy. Even if a fetus can't feel, it continually takes on and absorbs energy while in the womb.

My mother became pregnant with me during spring break of her freshman year of college. She was eighteen at the time and did her best to hide her pregnancy, but by July her body gave her away.

Later, she and I talked about the fear she felt—the fear of telling her parents and the fear of what she was going to do. She and my father decided to marry and keep me. Even though they made what I consider the right decision, all her emotions stayed with me as I gestated.

Everything about your birth mother affected your development. This symbiotic relationship goes well beyond the physical as you feel and internalize everything while floating in the amniotic fluid. The connection is only separated physically at birth.

Babies of women who abuse chemical substances are often born addicted to those same substances. The chemicals in the mother's blood run through the fetus. The physicality of the addiction cannot be denied.

When a baby is born, we look for the physical similarities to the mother and father. They don't have a developed personality yet, so their smile or the shape of their nose is what we're able to connect with.

YOUR MOTHER'S EMOTIONS ARE A PIECE OF THE PUZZLE

Researchers at the University of California San Francisco showed that the emotions felt by your mother become yours.

In the study, researchers separated a mother and child and exposed the mother to either happiness or stress. When the mother and child reunited, the emotions of the mother directly affected the heartbeat and reaction in the child. The more stressed the mother, the stronger the impact of the stress response on the infant.

This shows the direct impact on you as a child. Your mother's energy and emotions directly affected you, without her saying a word.

WHERE DOES YOUR FATHER FIT INTO ALL OF THIS?

In a 2013 study published in *ExtremeTech*, John Hewitt writes that through his work in mice studies, they showed that pups exhibit similar fears as that of their traumatized father. "The fear or at least the event that the experimenters chose to transfer was an association of the smell of a chemical known as acetophenone, an orange-like substance, which was paired with a slightly discomforting electric shock to their feet."

To reduce the influence of the environment, the pups were created via artificial semination. The only transfer of information and energy from the father was via the father's sperm.

When the pups' startle response was tested in response to different smells, they showed the biggest response to acetophenone. The pups never learned this smell was bad. They inherently knew it. This same response carried through to the grand-pups. Smell is one of our most powerful senses.

This has big implications for war veterans and their offspring. Their stressors affect your state of being, even without regular contact. If you continue to be exposed to familial stress, the impact grows exponentially. We've been fighting wars for centuries, on and off the battlefield.

---

*We've been fighting wars for centuries,
on and off the battlefield.*

Why Does an Infant Absorb What's Around Them?

You can look at birth order, sun signs, and other reasons for why people are the way they are, but what impacts you the most is the energetic environment during your early years as your brain, being, and emotions develop.

As an infant, you say very little with cognitive meaning. Your eyes are open, but you're essentially asleep. You have little judgment or critical thinking—no discernment, no filter, and no boundaries.

At birth, you were filled with empathy, with your heart wide open, full of love and trust.

Through the age of two, your brain waves were in a delta state, similar to sleeping or deep meditation.

You were completely dependent on the person caring for you. Trust was a basic foundation of your being. You didn't have to think about it. It was inherent.

Infants connect with adults through their tone of voice and by looking directly into their eyes. Interaction with your parents taught you to empathize, which tapped into your delta brain waves. During those initial months, your empathy either grows or fades.

The Gateway to Creativity

Delta brain waves continue until the age of two, at which point the energy moving through your brain increases speed, and your brain waves move into the state of theta.

In theta, you connect more to your inner world for a time of exploration, imagination, and accepting what you're told as true. You don't yet know the meaning of critical thinking.

The brain in theta is your gateway to learning, memory, and intuition. As an adult, it's the state of falling asleep or waking up, where you tap into thoughts and awareness beyond the logical mind.

Theta is the gateway into your subconscious, where you hold the energy and stories you've internalized. The biggest difference between theta and delta is the activation of the frontal lobe, which controls creativity and creative visualization.

WHAT SYNAPSES DID YOU CREATE?

As you grow, your autonomic nervous system (ANS) develops. The ANS regulates the body's unconscious actions and drives either the parasympathetic nervous system (our rest and digest functions) or the sympathetic nervous system (our fight or flight functions).

During your early years, synapses form pathways based on where your environment directs your energies. Only the used synapses and pathways survive into adulthood. A process called synaptic pruning eliminates your unused synapses.

Only the used synapses and pathways
survive into adulthood.

These may be the most important and formative years, when you begin to learn how you fit into the world. You're learning to express your thoughts and your feelings.

Your early environment sets the strength of the pathways through your ANS, which continue to develop into your late twenties.

The Pathways to Dreams

If in your early years, pathways formed for you to feel safe, stronger pathways to your sympathetic nervous system were created. Your pathways to creativity and visualization may have become secondary. You may not have felt safe to dream – then or now.

Being in a near-constant state of alert takes you away from the magic of living.

Everyone's childhood has some form of trauma and upset. That's part of growing up. When you take on the emotions and energy of those who raised you, you become uprooted from yourself. You are not able to fully explore your own landscape.

When my mother went into the hospital for three weeks, my brain was still in the theta wave state. I absorbed the world into my subconscious. I became silent to keep the peace, and I took on the fear from my environment. This formed the root of my old fears of abandonment.

The pathways to protection overtook the pathways to my dreams.

Loss and Feeling Powerless are Powerful Co-Conspirators

Everyone experiences loss. When you feel like people go away either literally or metaphysically, the pain becomes worse when you try to hold onto your dream.

When I was three and my mother was hospitalized for three weeks, she wasn't the same when she came back. I had a deep yearning for my mother as she was before. This created the need to give myself a semblance of control. My three-year-old self could never articulate this, yet the energy of it lived deep within my body and psyche.

I held on for a future that I didn't know was possible and that kept me tied to a dream and a relationship that no longer existed.

Control is a trauma response.

Control is a trauma response.

Dreams are like holding a dandelion—to loosely hold the stem while you gently blow on the seed head, allowing the seeds to float through the air and land where they may, and then you let go of the stem.

You're not meant to hold on for dear life. When you do, your hand is closed to the opportunity to hold another stem and blow more wishes into the consciousness of the universe.

Eventually, I realized why I had so much trouble letting go of the dream I had with my ex-husband, even after I walked away from the chaos of his alcoholism.

GET CURIOUS

Through conversations with my mother, I better understood the environment of my early years. She answered questions I didn't know I had, and that helped me put together pieces of my own puzzle.

Before these conversations, I needed to do a lot of healing to move beyond blame and feeling like a victim, into a state of curiosity.

Imagine open and honest conversations with your parent or family member that put together the pieces of your puzzle. The information you receive will be from their unique perspective, and that's okay. It will fill in some of the blanks with information you wouldn't otherwise have.

Do you remember feeling a certain way and not knowing why? Do you have memories of dreams, but you haven't figured out their meaning—like my dream of falling into a black hole?

What questions do you want to ask?

You want to believe the people you live with are good. Underneath everything, they are. God doesn't make mistakes. When you see someone beyond their stories, pain, and conflicts, you can connect with the divinity of who they are. It's their pain that spoke, not their true self.

FORMING CONCLUSIONS THAT STAY STUCK

Around the age of five, your brain waves quicken again and move into an alpha frequency. The analytical mind begins to form, and you begin to look at things with a more critical eye. You draw conclusions from your environment. The world inside your brain is as real as the world outside.

When you explore the definition of self, it refers to your individuality. As a child, you don't understand the concept of self. You look to adults to acknowledge your efforts and give you praise. This builds your self-esteem and begins the cycle of externalizing how you're seen and valued.

At this age, you're still you-centered, still without the discernment to detach from the tensions around you. In fact, you may feel like those issues are your responsibility.

By this age, you may have already started to silence yourself by shutting down your feelings. You might have begun to disassociate from yourself.

THIRTY SECONDS

At the end of my old street was an elementary school. I'd walk by it on my way to one of the nearby waterways where I'd birdwatch.

One day as I was in front of the school, a mother hurried behind her young son who was running toward the street. He was full of energy, about eighteen months old.

Behind her was her young daughter, walking with her backpack on her back.

The words out of the mother's mouth – "Hurry up. I'm trying to keep up with your brother. You're so lazy."

The whole situation unfolded in less than a minute.

When the young girl heard the last sentence, she stopped dead in her tracks.

The mother didn't see the impact to her daughter.

That last sentence. Those three words. "You're so lazy."

The mother and daughter may never remember this situation. Yet the energetic impact lingers on.

When we tell children they are something, they believe us. Then, they become it.

When we tell children they are something, they believe us.

Then, they become it.

My heart went out to both the mother and the daughter.

To the mother, for her to understand the impact of her words and for patience for her children.

How different the impact might have been if she had stopped at two sentences.

To the daughter, for her to understand that her mother was speaking out of frustration, for her to not become what her mother said she was, to not learn that negative behavior is the way to get attention. In short, to be free of the energetic impact of the situation and those words.

These situations and their energy stay with you. You feel a certain way and aren't sure where it comes from. When you're this young, you don't know any different than to believe what you're told.

Your children are listening, just as you did.

The words you choose are so important.

This is how patterns are created. Invisibly.

THE BODY EXPRESSES WHAT WE'RE NOT ABLE TO VERBALIZE

In third grade, I suddenly wasn't able to color within the lines. My nervous system attacked the drawing with the crayon in my hand. I expressed emotions I couldn't express in any other way. The teacher kept me in during recess to practice my coloring skills, which added to the shame I already felt from the sexual abuse I'd begun to experience.

I received no questions, no conversation, or exploration of the sudden change in my behavior. There was no why. I created safety within by adding a new level of silencing myself, even though the crayon on the paper said something very different.

I created safety within by adding
a new level of silencing myself.

While in middle school, I had chronic sore throats that began around the time I was challenged to color within the lines. I received course after course of Penicillin but my sore throats were never fully cured with drugs. I'd have temporary relief, then another round of medicine shortly thereafter. My words and grief were stuck in my throat, just as my nervous system had expressed itself through the lines on the coloring paper.

To this day, I can hear and feel the words of my abuser as he passed by me in our garage: "I'll kill you if you tell anyone." I froze in my tracks, unable to move, silenced on the spot.

I buried my shame so deep inside of me that I didn't know how to find my way out. I didn't know how to access all that I'd buried.

THE MIX OF CHILDHOOD

Childhood is often a mix of good and bad. You might experience exquisite love from your mother or father while also experiencing their rage, outbursts, or silence. Challenging episodes feel like you're swinging from one side of the pendulum to the other. What was true, and what was your experience? Both. And.

Your parents were living their lives, and you were a part of that, although you thought the world revolved around you. Your brain and subconscious play along with this.

In those early years, you didn't know the concept of expectations. If a parent was in the middle of something, you may have felt shut down. You may have felt not seen or heard because your parent was preoccupied. This isn't what you expected, which created a feeling of disconnect.

I lived a middle-class life in suburban neighborhoods, ate three meals each day, had snacks, celebrated birthdays with my choice of cake, climbed trees, rode my bike with abandon, and had lots of free time to explore. Nothing about it was extraordinary, and maybe that's the point.

When things just are, and life floats along, you don't pay a lot of attention. The highs and lows capture your attention. Few highs come to mind, but the lows energetically stick with you. The lows fill your imagination and subconscious with reasons as to what and why.

THE ROOT OF CODEPENDENCY

Rather than continuing with the beautiful intuitiveness and trust you were born with, you seek external validation and parts of them slip away.

As a child, when your environment doesn't give you the fulfillment that is inherently yours, you seek it elsewhere.

As a child, when your environment doesn't give you the fulfillment that is inherently yours, you seek it elsewhere.

This is the root of codependency.

Marketers feed into these feelings of lack. How long were your holiday or birthday wish lists?

Marketing messages taught you that you'll feel better when you have [insert material object here]. Eventually, those items need to be bigger or better.

THE ENERGY BEHIND THE CONNECTION

The word *codependence* is often associated with addiction and the relationship between two or more people. One person enables the other in their addiction. The word has a negative connotation because of our perception of what addiction looks like.

But codependence is something we're inherently born into. It's the natural state of depending on the people who raised you. Everything in this world is dependent on something else. There's nothing wrong with being dependent on another. That's how you make your way through the world.

The energy behind the connection tells the story. When you look to others to solve your own internal challenges or look to others to make you feel better, this creates a cycle of codependence that may not be healthy.

Codependence is different from co-creation. Co-creation is when another person brings insight, and you listen to your own internal knowing to find the answer already within you.

Consider codependence and co-creation as opposite ends of the spectrum. Co-creation taps into your intuition and your connection with Spirit. The more you look to others for your inspiration, the lower your ability to truly co-create.

THE LAYERS OF YOUR CAKE

Codependency and your stories are like the layers of your cake. Distraction is the icing. It covers what you don't want to see. Distraction is your addictions. You may distract yourself with other people's lives, drama, work, gardening, shopping, porn, eating, video games, social media, and sometimes even aches and pains within your body. You might have as many flavors of icing as layers to your cake.

Distraction is the icing.

When you don't know where you fit in the world, or in your own internal world, you seek things outside of yourself to make you feel better. If you've experienced any form of trauma, you may be fighting that old energy to feel safe.

This is where you live in a dichotomy. You can be fully connected to the external world, while experiencing a deep invisible void within. The noise of your stories creates the void. To turn off the noise, you create new layers of icing.

FAMILY LAYERS OF CAKE

Have you ever felt that if you don't talk about something, you can pretend it doesn't exist?

Have you ever questioned someone in the family about a situation, and they questioned you back rather than open up? They became defensive and took your questions personally, when you didn't mean it that way.

In the family dysfunction of silence, the other person may take your approaching them as a personal affront.

The original question doesn't get resolved. Everyone goes on guard, and a new layer of cake forms.

YOU KNOW, BUT YOU DON'T

If your parents waited until you were in bed to have an argument, you may still have taken in that energy. As a person sleeps, their brain waves move between alpha, theta, and delta during which REM occurs. During certain periods of deep dream state, your brain is awake to receive.

Parents can pretend that the kids don't know, and the youngsters may or may not be consciously aware, but their subconscious is turned on. They may wake up with feelings they can't express. They may not know where those feelings came from. Their parents act like nothing happened. This can put the children at odds with their logical mind.

This doesn't only happen when we're children. As an adult you might know something is happening, but you're kept in the dark. If you question it, you're told it isn't true. Think about a spouse having an affair, or whispers about friends getting together and you're not invited, or you're left out of the planning of major strategic moves at work.

In these cases, you know something is happening around you. You have an uneasy feeling. You know you know...but you don't. Your intuition is trying to speak to you.

This can feel like a divine conspiracy. It is, but not the way you think.

BEING A SILENT WITNESS

One of my former doctors grew up in the Ukraine where access to therapy wasn't readily available. People sat on buses or park benches and talked, not necessarily to each other but to have someone as a witness.

It was an opportunity to express how they felt to someone without judgment, someone who wouldn't react emotionally.

City parks now have chat benches or The Friendship Bench, a Canadian network. Numerous mental health and crisis hotlines are also available.

If you feel like no one is available to hear your words, creative options are available.

WHAT IS WAITING TO BE EXPRESSED?

Your Invitation: Explore what you have been waiting to express. Writing in a journal is a powerful and a somatic experience that helps move the energy within your body. If you don't have a safe place to keep your notes, you can write and tear the paper up into many small pieces, which itself can be cathartic.

Write a letter that expresses everything you've wanted to say, then don't send it. This practice gives a voice to your words and clears some of the layers of energy.

Go for a walk by yourself and have a conversation between yourself and someone else. Express everything you've wanted to say, how you felt, and what you wanted to hear from them.

Go swimming and yell under water. Yell into a pillow.

Find a Rage or Smash Room where you can smash old computer equipment with a bat. Physically move energy out of your body while you also express what you need to say. This is an incredibly empowering experience.

This is your personal purge. Tap into feeling like a victim and give yourself permission to feel the emotions you have bottled up—rage, anger, sadness, disbelief, betrayal and abandonment, to name a few.

Your feelings are unique to you, and no one ever has the right to invalidate or silence them. Remember to be gentle with yourself.

You will start to find who you are underneath. You will realize you weren't crazy. The thoughts and feelings you pushed aside were real, but they've been stunted. As you explore each new layer, you may find the walls melt around you as you find deeper trust within your heart.

The thoughts and feelings you pushed aside were real.

Be careful you don't stay stuck in the old space. Connect in a way you may not have in the past. See it, feel it, clear it, and then choose to move beyond. Find a balance between rebellion and numbness.

CHAPTER 4
THE (UN)CONSCIOUS DECEPTION IN SILENCE

"The cruelest lies are often told in silence."
~ Robert Louis Stevenson

COMPETITION AND THE PUSH UP THE LADDER

In my twenty-seven years on Wall Street, the culture expected you to want more and counted you as lazy if you weren't playing the game. To be happy and not pushing to climb the corporate ladder was odd. Those who pushed ahead received prize assignments. People who didn't push were less likely to be listened to and often were cast aside even when they were a key part of keeping the business running.

The people you work with play into many of your unresolved emotions from childhood.

COMPETITION AND SELF-WORTH

Bosses and colleagues will compete against your talents, minimize your contribution, or take credit for your work, so you won't outshine them. When this happens, the trusted become the untrusted, and you may no longer want to share your brilliant ideas.

When you shine your light, the discomfort and darkness within others may come out. You may feel ostracized where you feel safer to not share, not speak, and not shine, so you can fit in. You don't want to be singled out.

How many times have you asked yourself the question, "What do I need to do to get ahead?" That's a rhetorical question because the rules are rarely divulged, and if you're not playing the game, you're out. What's in your way isn't always what you think it is.

I began to see how the energies of competition and self-worth play into each other and may conflict.

When competition is based on feeding the ego, the drive to compete may take you further away from who you are while you're feeding your self-esteem.

THE PAST IN THE PRESENT

"You were such a horrible child because you were so sick."

At a young age, Cindy was labeled as sick and angry. When she became a client, she still heard an echo of her mother and her siblings.

Cindy's story was playing out in her business, her family relationships, and her relationship with her husband. She struggled to find happiness, and couldn't understand why she was hitting a wall in her business. Her childhood sickness had a direct effect on her financial wealth and day-to-day freedom and success, but she hadn't made the connection.

Her unexpressed anger continued to affect her life as an adult. Potential clients weren't saying yes, and she didn't understand why. She was also experiencing continued illnesses, and doctors couldn't find out why.

You can't help but perpetuate what you grew up around.

You can't help but perpetuate what you grew up around.

Cindy is just one example of what I see with many of my clients.

"It was so hard raising you," doesn't allow for healing. It doesn't create a clean space between you and the other person, even when you've done a lot of work to heal.

Cindy came to me at her wit's end and finished our work together feeling more herself than she ever had. Through our work together, we cleared the energies connected to her old stories. She was able to see her family in a new light and powerfully move forward with a new perspective.

She was no longer tied to the labels of her childhood illnesses or the confusion those labels created in her life.

Your voice and speaking your truth are the keys to living a vibrant life.

WE ALL WANT TO BE HEARD

As individuals, we haven't been heard for a long time. We have so much noise running around inside our brains and body that we don't have the capacity to listen. It goes beyond the idea, if you won't listen to me, then I won't listen to you.

We're so deeply closed off to ourselves, we're so disconnected from what we know within ourselves to be true that the marketers and politicians seem to have won.

Do any of these scenarios feel familiar, particularly in business or politics?

- ∞ It's okay to speak up, but don't say anything original. You must affirm the position.

- ∞ Fall in line and be a cog in the machine. We don't have time to consider your questions. Curiosity isn't welcome.

- ∞ Talking in a meeting while others look at their phone, read an email on their computer, swivel their chair to indicate their boredom, or cut you off mid-sentence.

- ∞ The boss tells you that they'll be presenting your ideas or work.

If you've experienced any of these, how might that shutdown feeling be similar to your younger years?

SUBTLY SILENCED

You've probably asked someone for something and received a turn in the other direction instead. A person might try to exert power over you by giving you the cold shoulder, by ignoring your request, or by denying the conversation. They know if they listen to you, they will have to make a choice about whether to be honest or not.

But what if their behavior is more insidious? What if they are giving you the proverbial grin-fuck, where a person nods yes, but they have no intention of helping you or acknowledging a situation between you?

The bandwidth of the person hearing you may directly correspond to their capacity to listen.

Adding to the quandary, the person on the other end of your conversation may be afraid of how you will perceive them, that the topic is somehow a reflection on them.

They might try to silence you via the clearing of their throat, a raised eyebrow, or a look over the top of their eyeglasses.

ACTIONS SPEAK LOUDER THAN WORDS

A person may say yes to a conversation, but if they're going through the motions to appease you, you feel incomplete, although you can't put your finger on the problem.

The person said all the right things, but their energy didn't ring true. You sense something more, while questioning yourself about what you're missing. This is more subtle than a person outright saying, "I didn't push you down the stairs. You slipped and fell."

Are they consciously deceiving you? Perhaps. They may have agreed to the conversation, so you'll go away. In this instance, they would be more honest if they said, "Fuck off," because then you are clear on exactly where you stand.

ACCEPTED AT WHAT COST?

Every group has a leader. Their nod in favor of a person or an idea gives approval for the others to say yes. That yes can sometimes feel like it seals your fate.

And all done without saying a word.

To receive the yes, or a promotion, means you're accepted. But accepted at what cost? What part of yourself did you dim in order to be accepted?

Competing against co-workers, pushing people out of the way, manipulating those around you, and playing a game to climb another rung on the ladder doesn't resolve your old issues. It may actually make things harder because you now have less you can honestly share.

When you are done, you may have more money and more prestige, but in exchange you harden your edges and give up part of yourself. Is it worth it?

It's time to figure out a new game with new rules and new people to trust. Restart the cycle of asking, "Where do I fit in?

It's time to figure out a new game with new rules.

DODGEBALL

The energy from your younger years can follow you into your adult life, where you believe money is power. Using money and power for status feels like a continuous game of dodgeball and sibling rivalry all wrapped up into one.

Life isn't meant to be a game of dodgeball with forced competition, quick elimination of the weakest, and the humiliation of being picked off early.

The people you work for and hang out with will play into many of your unresolved emotions from childhood. One of the biggest may be self-worth.

How much of yourself do you share?

Is it safe to be heard and shine?

How much do you have to do?

How much of yourself do you have to give away to be seen?

Will you always dodge invisible energy you can't define?

Our Logical Mind Plays Games

- ∞ We compare—So-and-so is already doing this, so why would anyone want to listen to me?
- ∞ We settle—It's better than nothing. It's not terrible; it's okay. It's shitty, but it's all I have.
- ∞ It's unconscious—I don't deserve better than this.

You're taught to play these games that feed into your doubt and thus to turn yourself off.

No one is meant to move through life feeling alone, yet that's exactly what happens. We turn off the people around us as self-protection, but that cuts us off from the exact thing we crave.

What's the Energy of Your Social Media?

Look at your last dozen social media posts. Do they have an energy of fighting an old battle? Have you shared a message of hope for yourself and for others? When you post about a challenging situation, the energy of your words shows your perception of the world.

When do you stop recycling messages of fear and suppression?

---

*When do you stop recycling messages
of fear and suppression?*

WHAT'S THE PERSPECTIVE ON YOUR LENS?

You can't change what was or wasn't provided for you. But if you want to be happier, to move out of the old pain and stories that silence you today, choose a new lens to view your past.

This doesn't mean shitty things didn't happen, and you have nothing to heal. Few adults escape feeling silenced or alone. I was a poster child of feeling hurt and betrayed until I got real with myself.

This doesn't mean seeing the world through rose-colored glasses. You're seeing with new clarity through a new lens.

In the early months of my travels in 2019, I came upon a couple on the beach in Tybee Island, Georgia. The husband was experiencing a lot of pain in his lower back. I did some quick energy work with him. Intuitively, I asked him about work. He was in the middle of a big job transition with many challenges. We connected his pain to those challenges. What came through was for him to focus on what he did want to create, not on what he didn't want.

Almost immediately the lightbulb went off for him. He saw things from a new perspective. He'd been struggling with where he came from and acting from that energy. When he shifted his perspective, his body also shifted.

CHANGE THE NARRATIVE

Few of us have a lot of control over how we were raised and by whom. We often feel like a victim of circumstances. But as an adult, you can choose to change your narrative. This is what Cindy did, and not only did her relationships and business thrive, but she also gained new levels of peace. She was no longer triggered by her mother's narrative.

As an adult, you can choose to change your narrative.

Like Cindy, you can listen to and see with your soul.

CONNECT WITH THE NOISE

Even if the majority of your silencing comes from within, you can still heal.

Awareness is key. Without awareness, old patterns keep going.

Hauntings are echoes that are waiting to be heard.

Your Invitation: You've already begun to explore where you've felt silenced, your family tree, and what's waiting to be expressed. You're now invited to pull these together, to see the deeper patterns, and to identify what you'll no longer take on.

On a sheet of paper, write what you want to experience in the first column. Write how you're not experiencing them in a second column. What's the gap between the two columns?

When you explore the gap, look at what you don't want or are no longer willing to tolerate.

Some examples include how you feel drawn into other people's drama, gossip, comparison, bigotry, and judgment or feeling responsible for someone else's happiness.

Doing this, you may discover patterns from your younger years.

As you explore and expand, this will continue to evolve. As you become aware of the layers of your cake, you create the connection from then to now, so you can clear it.

Here is an opportunity to make an agreement with yourself, a sacred pact to unwind, let go, and create a new story, layer by layer.

CHAPTER 5

QUIETING THE MYTHS & LISTENING TO YOUR SOUL'S WHISPERS

"It takes courage to grow up and become who you really are."
~ e e cummings

WHY YOU CAN'T CREATE A NEW STORY

Does the following sound familiar?

∞ You can't change the past, so what's the point?

∞ You're not there anymore, so it doesn't matter.

Or perhaps you've told yourself:

∞ I have it under control. I'm good.

∞ I don't have the time.

∞ I did therapy, or I've already done all the things.

∞ Nothing worked in the past, so why bother?

∞ This will work for others but not for me.

Or you may believe that if you're different, you won't be accepted.

∞ People will reject me if I change.

∞ Other people's opinions help me see who I am.

These are all misconceptions. In reality, they describe why you are stuck.

They describe why you are stuck.

How many of these have you told yourself? Do you still believe some of them?

As with most misconceptions, many were created in a very different time and came down through the generations.

It's like the story about why the meatloaf recipe calls for the pan to be a certain size, only to find out that it was based on the size of the pan your great-grandmother used.

Prior generations didn't have agency, tools, capacity, or support. They also didn't understand the mind-body-spirit connection as deeply as we do now.

Misconceptions provided reasons to avoid the healing journey and bypass your power.

PERSPECTIVE AND TIME

We built our lives around logic and doing. Connecting with self is a luxury, especially when we add the expectation of instant gratification.

You can't physically change past events, but you can change your perspective and the energy connected with those events.

Time always seems to expand when something feels important. When you say you don't have time, or you have things under control, fear is often the reason. The ego speaks from the old place because you feel safe where you are.

Fear can be thought of in two ways. The first – false expectations appearing real. The second – feel everything and rise. Every day, moment by moment, you have a choice of how you show up.

Fear keeps you from change.

Ask yourself, *Are the people around me truly supporting my growth, or do they want to keep me where I am so they feel safe and comfortable?*

Many of my clients come to me after exhausting all other options. Those who are ready to move through their old fears will make tremendous changes in their lives.

THE CONDITIONING THAT COMES FROM THE MYTHS AND MISCONCEPTIONS

These myths have evolved since well before the automation and machination of our world.

When you see how myths apply in your life, how they form the stories embedded in your being, and how much noise they create, you can finally find the truth underneath the myths. Those myths silenced you. You used them to silence yourself.

Those myths silenced you.
You used them to silence yourself.

When your ego knows you want to change, its automatic response is to keep you safe where you are. You may ask, *What's the point?* and go on with your day. This is the unconscious battle between your ego and your soul.

Make conscious choices about how you live and move about the world.

As an adult, how you tell your stories is solely up to you.

If you allow the noise to win, you mute out your soul.

WHERE ARE YOU?

Until you understand how you arrived at where you are, you will remain silenced, and little will change.

Your ego may step in and tell you, *I should have my shit together by now. This is just how I am; it's just how it is. Fuck it.* This is more misconception. You're exactly where you're meant to be, right now, even if it feels uncomfortable.

WHERE ARE YOU ON YOUR TO-DO LIST?

Your to-do list may include a loved one or family member. If you find yourself doing more for them than they do for themselves, that's a signal to step back from a layer of your cake. When you help someone to the detriment of yourself, neither of you benefits.

Many women were raised to make sure everyone around them was okay first. Their leftover time was for them. Codependent patterns made sure the outside of you was okay before taking care of your insides. Few people were taught the importance of self-care.

Your mind may claim you don't care, but you actually do. You connected with this book for a reason. Don't allow your mind to turn off your wants by saying no to yourself when you want to say yes. Living an intellectualized life will silence you and your emotions. This, too, is where you might talk a good game and still do nothing.

Growing up feeling silenced leads you to want to control the world. Feeling like you have control gives you comfort. Fear of where you're headed may feel overwhelming.

Open spaces allow you to play. The things for you to look at don't come to you all at once. If you don't know where to start, ask Spirit for guidance about where to focus for your highest good.

THE FEAR OF LOSING WHO YOU ARE

I have stories of sexual abuse, of abandonment, of the why's for my drug abuse and unhealthy relationships. Through these stories, I clung to my label as a survivor and the proof of how I thrived in chaos.

My stories focused on how the world made me feel that way. They justified my feelings and defined who I was.

The thought of letting go of my stories terrified me. My stories were my identity. I'd finally "figured" out who I was and where I fit in. I'd found my "people." Who would I be without them?

Deep down, though, we never lose the connection to who we truly are. We need to shed the stories and the labels to get clear on our truth.

We need to shed the stories and the
labels to get clear on our truth.

In reality, I got tired of those old stories and the energy they carried. I got tired of chaos.

Letting go is like the transformation of the caterpillar to the butterfly.

BECOMING A BUTTERFLY

The story of the caterpillar turning into the butterfly appears in many stories. The actual transformation happens when the caterpillar turns into goo. The old self dissolves except for core parts, which form the basis of the butterfly. While the butterfly looks very different, its DNA remains the same, carried forward via imaginal cells.

These imaginal cells are at first experienced as an attack on the caterpillar, and its immune system kicks in with protection. Eventually, the imaginal cells take over, and produce the raw material that forms the basis of the butterfly.

Think of the caterpillar as your ego, the layers of your cake. Letting go of old beliefs is like your imaginal cells attacking your ego.

In the imaginal cells are discs that contain the gut, the tracheal tubes for breathing, and part of the central nervous system. In your human self, this aligns with your solar plexus and heart energy centers and the core of your physical being.

The gut is your connection with your higher self and intuition. Your capacity to breathe is a core piece of your existence. The same with the beating of your heart. Your central nervous system is your foundation, who you are beneath the old layers. Love and belonging are at the center of your being.

The caterpillar doesn't question its place in the world, and it doesn't question the process. To become a butterfly, the caterpillar sheds what it no longer needs so it can step into the next phase of its life.

To become a butterfly, the caterpillar sheds what it no longer needs so it can step into the next phase of its life.

This is your time to uncover what's hidden.

This is where you get to explore. Step away from your logical mind. Connect with your heart and your intuition. If judgment comes up, acknowledge and thank it. Allow your feelings to flow through you. Don't get attached to them because they're simply information. The deeper you go, the more informed you'll be.

THE SILENCING OF YOUR SOUL

When you don't choose your light, you choose your misconceptions and stay stuck in the past. As you leave your internalized stories unacknowledged, you dull who you are and accept who you think you are. Rather than walking through the dark to come out on the other side of the tunnel, you take life in bite-sized pieces.

Do you distract yourself because you're afraid to see what you're not doing with your life? Sometimes, numbing is easier than seeing the possibilities before you. What if your dream doesn't happen? More disappointment. So instead, you turn to binge-watching and shopping. Those are small enough to handle. Bite size.

But what if your dream did happen? Would those emotions and feelings be more than you feel comfortable with? This is where we mind-fuck ourselves and keep ourselves small.

WHAT DOES SILENCING YOUR SOUL DO ON A DEEPER LEVEL?

You close your heart to create a sense of safety away from your old trauma. As you fight through a sea of unknowns, the ego keeps you attached to the knowns—your stories. Trying to shut off the noise, you lose the very connection you seek, the connection with self.

Trying to shut off the noise, you lose the very connection you seek, the connection with self.

The inner critic comes out. Your heart may stay hardened, and you may find yourself in a never-ending cycle of self-sabotage. The ego takes over and plays into the patterns of judgment and being overly hard on yourself. This takes you away from your creativity. So, not only are your words unsafe, but you aren't safe to express them.

This idea may make you feel defensive. When you're ready, look at it from a different perspective. Look beyond the external world and into the deeper world of who you are. Who are you underneath all the layers, the definitions, the perceptions, and the stories? Take off your mask and take a good look.

WHEN DISASSOCIATION NO LONGER SERVES YOU

Without realizing it, I used disassociation as a powerful form of protection and as a safety mechanism. When I was younger, disassociation protected me from what I couldn't process. It splintered off parts of me.

At that time, I sometimes came across as unemotional.

I did care, but I wasn't able to access the parts of me that I'd shut down years earlier. I showed as much emotion as I was capable of at the time.

Life felt easier when it was logical. When you don't want to see something, disassociating feels like control.

Then, life cracked me open.

In reality, your soul can never be touched, but you don't feel that way when a tidal wave hits you. As an adult, I had to learn to be with my feelings and no longer silence them.

For a long time, I felt a deep emptiness. I didn't know how to fill the void, so I looked outside of myself for validation.

I was confused about how to fill the void, so I reached in the wrong direction for years. The easy answers of work, gardening, and lots of distractions didn't make my life easier. They only prolonged the journey and increased the pain. I needed to pull the lost pieces of myself back inside me.

THE DIVINE CONSPIRACY

Is a divine conspiracy taking you away from yourself? In reality, no. It's not a conspiracy. Major things happen in life to help you connect more deeply beyond your stories.

We're conditioned to get back on the horse. We're taught to push through whatever's in front of us and go back to the way life was before.

What if you aren't meant to go backward or stay stagnant? What if the challenge in front of you is meant to help you shed what's holding you back?

HEALING AND SANDPAPER

When we begin to sense something is wrong with a situation, it can feel like 0000 steel wool rubbing against your skin. It's a little annoying, but you can ignore it.

It starts to rub some more. The situation begins to take up mental space, but not so much that you're not able to swipe left and continue to ignore it. Now, it feels more like 00 steel wool. A little coarse, yet still tolerable.

Then the situation goes beyond your mental space, and it starts to get into your emotions.

When you think about the situation, your body has a visceral reaction. Even with a lot of mental energy, you can still swipe left and ignore the situation. The rub feels more like a fine grit sandpaper.

Next, you begin to feel like you can't get away from it, and you can't swipe left. The situation takes up a lot more of your space, mentally, emotionally, energetically, and physically. It feels like medium grit sandpaper. Metaphorically, the wound's been opened.

Emotionally and energetically, it's exhausting to be in this space. It's a tug of war to subconsciously fight off an old story coming to the surface because it wants to go.

Now, the coarse grit sandpaper comes out. You can no longer ignore what's going on. Every cell in your body is activated, and you must make a change. You can't stand it anymore. You make the decision that it's time to physically separate yourself because the coarse grit sandpaper is rubbing against all aspects of your being.

You decide you're tired of the old narrative. The old story doesn't fit any more. You have to let it go.

CLEARING KARMA

What you bring from the past directly influences the present.

The more attached you are to your stories, the more karma you create both in this life and also future lives. Some of what we experience in this life is based on our past lives.

In his book *Many Lives, Many Masters*, Brian L Weiss, MD, goes deep into the blend of science and metaphysics, telling how he used past-life therapy to help patients heal beyond their current life experiences.

Everyone has multiple life lessons to experience while here on earth. When you look underneath the specifics of your life experiences, you will find a common theme.

When you look underneath the specifics of your life experiences, you will find a common theme.

In your last moments of life, do you want to be attached to your stories of pain, hurt, betrayal, and abandonment? Are these the energies you want to carry into your next life?

Healing opens space within and around you. It frees you of the old blinders. When you heal, you're able to clear the karma of the past.

Many Native American and indigenous tribes believe that when we heal, the work goes back seven generations and forward for seven. We get to clear the energies for our ancestors who couldn't heal their trauma, and clear space for the next generations.

The religion of my upbringing gave me two options: heaven or hell. They had no way to heal the stories I carried inside. A spiritually conscious path has opened many avenues for me to move beyond the energies of the old stories.

A SACRED BATH

One night, as I soaked in the tub, I looked at the form of my legs, my hips, and my belly through the water. A whisper came through, *I can no longer ignore that I'm here.*

I realized that in some respects, I was still going through the motions of life. I was doing things to keep myself busy. I had a lot of projects, but I wasn't fully connected to my heart.

I also realized that for much of my life I was going through the motions and following the rules to create the life I thought I was supposed to create. Being in a new location shifted many things, but it didn't shift the deeper lessons I still had to learn.

HAPPINESS VS. JOY

Happiness came to me through the satisfaction of doing all the things I thought I was supposed to do—career, the house, the husband.

Logically, I know happiness is fleeting, but I was still driven to do more. Happiness silenced the joy that wanted to come through.

Happiness silenced the joy that wanted to come through.

My thought, *I can no longer ignore that I'm here,* became the driver to look for the joy I was born with, the joy nothing could take away, the joy I'd disconnected from because of all the stories I told myself, the stories I'd internalized.

With joy came responsibility. *I can no longer ignore that I'm here* was a wake-up call to my connection with myself, with my heart, and ultimately with God.

CRACKING OPEN

Not long after the bath, I came upon a jet-black kitten on the river walk near me, a beautiful little creature full of love. The first time I saw her she'd just caught a bird. She turned around, looked at me with her big yellow-green eyes, and went right back to the bird. She was obviously very hungry.

A few days later, I saw her again and called her over. She was so happy for human connection, and I petted her for about fifteen minutes. As I tried to step away, she kept wrapping herself around my ankles, not wanting me to leave. I gently broke free and cried as I walked away. Further along, I looked back. She sat in the middle of the walkway, staring at me.

How could anyone abandon something so beautiful and sweet?

I realized I'd done the same thing to myself. We do this with our younger aspects that want to be seen, heard, and loved, just like that kitten. Sometimes, the fear of facing the pain keeps us away from the very thing our heart craves.

The fear of facing the pain keeps us away
from the very thing our heart craves.

When I worked on Wall Street, I thought I had it all together. On the outside, I did.

The many rescue pets that lived with me showed me uncondi-tional love when I didn't know how to love myself.

WALKING AWAY

Walking away from the kitten cracked my heart open. So much love was available for me, the most important from myself and Spirit. But when our hearts are closed off, we pour our attention to things outside of ourselves. Our pets are a direct reflection of our capacity to experience and receive love, even when we can't see it for ourselves.

I realized my struggle to leave the kitten was like the chains of codependency that held me down. It was time to go deeper within. This was the beginning of walking away from my old life in a whole new way.

THE GIFT OF LITTLE MOMENTS

That kitten took me deep within my heart. I needed to mourn—for my adult self, for my younger self, and for all the parts of me I'd given away. As I did this, splintered pieces of my Self began to come back, the parts of me that saw it was safe to return.

Sometimes, it's not a 9-11 event, or ending a marriage, los-ing a job, or an illness that brings you to your knees. In lit-tle moments, Spirit will give you opportunities to go into your heart. When you're open to receive, you have a choice of how to move through the experience.

BOUNDARIES AS PROTECTION

The kitten was frightened around people. She stayed away until she grew weary. This is exactly how humans react. We put up boundaries as a form of protection when the world doesn't feel safe.

WE'RE NEVER TRULY ABANDONED

I wasn't able to take her home. For weeks, I didn't see her. While she may have felt abandoned, other walkers fed her and gave her a padded cat carrier to sleep in. She had many looking after her.

I was never truly abandoned either, although I felt like I was. None of us is. I abandoned myself, just as I abandoned my relationship with Spirit. I created my own separation from myself and from God.

This was part of my divine conspiracy because it opened me to what's truly important. It wasn't the career, the house, or the trappings around me. Spirit was always there, waiting for me.

One morning, I came upon a woman, and we talked about this beautiful kitten. She devised a plan to catch her, take her for a health check, and have her spayed. Soon, the kitten was relocated to her family farm in Idaho.

HEARING YOUR SOUL THROUGH CRISIS

While you might feel you can manage or control a situation, no one wants to admit to numbing themselves beyond what's acceptable.

A crisis comes along to wake you up, to bring you to a point where you can't ignore that you're here. Everything around you will shut down to bring you into focus. Most of the time, you focus on the crisis, and when you get through it, you think you're done.

A crisis comes along to wake you up.

I did this through many events, including 9-11 and the end of my marriages. Spirit stripped things away until there was nothing left but me.

If you've done this, you have an opportunity to go back and take a deeper look.

Spirit is always waiting to help you with the question, *What else is here for me to see or explore?*

PERPETUATING PAIN

You can be like a dog with a bone, not willing to let go until you receive an apology or an acknowledgment. You can push and want people to feel as much pain as you've felt. All that does is keep you stuck in a never-ending loop, which hurts the other people involved and perpetuates your pain.

Many don't want to get out of their loop. It's part of their subconscious patterns, as I did for many years.

I was attached to my stories. I felt the way I did because of someone else, what they did or didn't do, and how "they" made me feel.

A GIFT IN STORY FORM

Back in 2017, I was at a day of seminars for AA and Al-Anon. I went to an AA session, since it was unfamiliar to me (Al-Anon were my peeps). During the AA session, a man told the group his story about when he was a teenager. His father had pushed him to do drugs with him, including heroin.

I led an ACOA (Adult Children of Alcoholics) session right after, and this same man shared this same story. Almost verbatim.

That was a huge lightbulb moment for me.

I heard many stories repeated in the Al-Anon meetings I attended, but I felt a different energy this day. I saw things from a different perspective.

I saw how attached this man was to his story. Even though he'd done a lot of work, he didn't want to let it go, or he didn't know how to.

This is how we subconsciously keep ourselves stuck.

I also saw how attached I'd been. This man telling his story was a true gift and a catalyst for me.

I realized how allowing my stories to define me created a cycle of not liking my life.

Allowing my stories to define me
created a cycle of not liking my life.

I decided I wanted something different.

DECIDING TO LET GO

Deciding to let go is an active choice that requires no one but you.

When you want to move beyond feeling stuck, the path will begin to form for you.

Energies are attached to your stories, invisible energies that aren't logical. They drive you, your decisions, and how you show up in the world.

When you stop expecting something from someone who isn't capable of giving it to you, you take back your power.

Sometimes, you feel like you could wait a thousand years for an apology and still never receive it. An apology would require them to explore their own shame. They may not be able to admit their wrongdoing, or they may not be emotionally able.

You will never win a battle against someone else's internalized shame.

You will never win a battle against someone else's internalized shame.

When you don't want to feel or see something, you find power in disassociating.

The thing is, sometimes people want to stay angry or hurt. They've identified with feeling that way for so long that they don't know how to let it go. The layers of their cake serve them. Some people don't want to heal.

You have the choice to sit in silence and wait, or you can acknowledge yourself, acknowledge the situation, and release yourself.

We haven't been taught how to apologize or how to communicate in this way, especially if at a young age our emotions were shut down or minimized. Few of us experienced true apologies from adults. They didn't think they needed to. We learn to articulate based on the examples around us.

Receiving a true apology is rare.

As Buddha said, "Holding onto anger is like drinking poison and expecting the other person to die."

WHERE DO YOU STILL SEEK AN APOLOGY?

Your Invitation: Rather than expecting an apology from someone else, give it to yourself. What do you want to hear? How will you feel when you hear it? You're invited to speak those words to yourself. Record them and listen as many times as you need, until you feel complete.

This process is active. It's contemplative and forward looking. This is where you find your voice and speak your truth for yourself, even if you're the only one to hear it.

Take this opportunity to look at the deeper why. See people as they are, not as you want them to be. This is also where you begin to free yourself.

Even if you don't believe that person would ever say what you'd like to hear, you can choose whether to let go or not.

CHAPTER 6

HEALING IN SILENCE & THE POWER OF BEING YOUR OWN WITNESS

"Over time your consciousness becomes awake within itself. The silent witness within saturates and illuminates the mind so that it does not look to the past or the future for fulfillment. It experiences peace and freedom within itself in every moment."
~ Deepak Chopra

DEEPENING CONNECTION

I realized ghosts existed in the house I'd shared with my ex-husband. Something was missing, and I knew I wasn't going to find it there. In January, 2019, I sold my house and went on the road. For the first time in thirty years, I had no pets, no partner, no rent, and no mortgage.

What incredible freedom to be completely unattached. It was the beginning of deeper freedom from the old ties and rules. Society defines our success by the things we have—the car, the house, the job, the partner—and they're all external.

I traveled for eight months. I met amazing people, and I explored on my own timeline. After some speaking engagements in Texas, I visited dozens of hot springs. Something magical happened when I was in communion with the minerals of the earth while also bathing in her waters.

As I headed into New Mexico, I wanted to connect with spiritual sites. On Easter Sunday, I visited Carlsbad Caverns. As I explored the formations hidden in the darkness of the earth, I felt like I was in church. But this time I felt no judgment, only beauty in the quiet. When I walked into the Big Room, my feeling was verified in the formation known as Top of the Cross.

DISENTANGLING FROM THE LAYERS

My travels included hikes to shrines, to caves, and to a medicine wheel at the top of a mountain. I visited a Benedictine monastery where I attended the monk's noontime chant. I sat at a shrine hidden in a cave on the backside of a small town. I walked many labyrinths and experienced a full moon meditation at a Buddhist temple.

These places of solace and peace had no rules and judgment about who I was or of the church of my upbringing. It brought me to new levels of surrender as I opened myself to receive.

This wasn't receiving in the old sense, such as if you were happy, you got a reward. Or you were happy because you received a reward.

This was about receiving the truths I hadn't been able to see, or that I hadn't wanted to see. The layers of icing on my own cake began to melt, and I didn't have to eat them. I felt at peace.

TRANSACTIONAL VALIDATION

My perception of receiving was based on what I knew from science. For every action, there's an equal and opposite reaction.

I'd worked hard for accolades, promotions, and raises. I'd done what I thought others wanted me to do, so they would see me and accept me. I made their lives easier, so they'd stay and I wouldn't be alone.

Relationships always had a transaction involved. With each transaction, I gave more and more of myself away. I silenced my very being in order to receive validation.

With each transaction,
I gave more and more of myself away.

One of my clients held deep anger and resentment towards his parents, because he was never able to prove himself enough to be accepted by his family. He became the comedian of the family. That helped him feel accepted, but he lost the connection with himself and couldn't feel proud of his own achievements. This disconnect carried into adulthood.

During our work, his father became ill, and my client wanted to move beyond their old pattern. He healed aspects of his younger self and also healed his relationship with his father before his father passed. My client could finally play in both his personal and professional life away from his old transactional pattern as he authentically shared himself.

The Fallacy of Tough Love

A few years before my travels, one of my first coaches yelled at me during a group call and said, "You're not open to receive." She said it in a way that stopped me in my tracks.

Tough love added to my internalized shame and could never move my dial forward. Her approach fit into my old pattern of feeling small and unsafe to speak. Her attempt to jolt me into new awareness did the exact opposite. Although, looking back now, I realize her assessment was right

---

Tough love added to my internalized shame.

Tough love will rarely open us up to see the beauty before us.

What Does It Mean to Be Open to Receive?

To receive is to open to what the universe provides, without expectation. We've been taught to power our way through the world, that a result is supposed to come out of our efforts. Yes, you may receive a paycheck, but that's based on an agreement.

To receive is to trust that what's meant for you will show up, and you don't have to earn it. To receive is to move beyond the wants and will of the ego, where you open to the whispers of intuition and Spirit, to take action without Spirit having to sneak through a crack in the window with a 2x4.

The Grace of Cancer

Not long after my experience with the kitten, I was diagnosed with breast cancer. Rather than seeing cancer as a scourge within my body, as society and the medical profession would have me to see it, I saw it as a gift of grace.

I came back to my connection with God and with myself. Not the God of my upbringing, but Spirit who's always been there, guiding me, even when everything felt dark. The divine conspiracy brought me deeper messages from Spirit.

The divine conspiracy helped me to step away from the fear I embodied at a young age, to understand what was underneath my stories, and to heal my internalized energies. I came back to who I truly am and connected with the joy within my heart.

I realized that I had everything I needed to heal this disconnection of health. What was in my body was created when I was still on Wall Street. By focusing on everything but me, I'd lost the connection to myself and who I was.

I took my body for granted.

As I made decisions, I could have played into the fear of the disease, but to do that would have continued to play into the fear that drove my life. With the fear came unnecessary noise that would have kept me disconnected from myself.

I stepped into deeper levels of trust and forgiveness for myself. Even in my darkest moments, I've never been as alone as I sometimes felt.

THE CATCH-22 OF HELP

When you feel like you can't ask anyone for help, Spirit still waits and listens. This means more than putting your life in someone else's hands expecting them to heal your sorrows, which is the codependent matrix. Ask for guidance from deep within your heart and open yourself to receive the whisper of an answer without judgment or expectation. Then take action.

That beautiful little black kitten was such an incredible gift for me. When I asked how anyone could abandon something so beautiful and loving and sweet, I saw deeper layers of myself.

We're all mirrors for each other. The message *I can no longer ignore that I'm here* meant I could no longer ignore my connection with God. God lives within my heart, and the kitten was the path inside.

We're all mirrors for each other.

There's a saying, "The longest journey you will make in your life is from your head to your heart," attributed to Rumi and Sufism, also to the Sioux Indians.

Your heart will truly guide you. We're now seeing how powerful the heart is, as part of the scientific community considers it your real brain. If you don't trust your heart because of the hurts or because you were taught to doubt yourself, your thoughts, feelings, or emotions, you can feel like you're in a catch-22.

SEEING THE PERFECTION

I took a while to see how all this played out. When things happened in my life, I couldn't always express the intricacies of my emotions and reactions. I wasn't always conscious of what I was doing. I expressed myself the only way I knew how. The result reflected the deep level of silencing in my family that goes back many generations.

While I didn't see things then, as an adult I understand how old emotions continue to affect my life and my decisions. As a child, I didn't feel in control of my emotions. As an adult, I am.

I also see the perfection of all of this. It brought me to where I am now, although the healing journey was painful and challenging at times.

Seeing my part in causing unnecessary pain to myself and others was the hardest part. The pain I pushed onto others caused a wall that kept them from seeing or hearing me. I created my own cycle of silencing.

I created my own cycle of silencing.

THE CHALLENGE WITH FORGIVENESS

I now know that my stepbrother acted out of his anger and emotions for reasons that are only his to tell.

Moving through a situation goes beyond forgiveness because forgiveness puts one person above the other and keeps you stuck in victim energy.

When you tell someone you forgive them from the perspective of lording over them, you still have energy to clear. When you truly forgive someone, you are clearing the energy within yourself as well as clearing the way for all involved to own their path.

WHO ABSOLVES WHO?

You aren't responsible to make another person see what they've done. You do not have the power to absolve them. This is solely between them and God. And on some level, they're already fully aware of this.

One night in a dream, my stepbrother came to me and asked for absolution. In the dream, I told him I'd forgiven him, that

I held no further ill-will toward him, but that only God could absolve him. He needed to do his own work to come to peace within himself.

Carolyn Myss talks about forgiveness and sin. It's one thing to say you're sorry, yet many times those are just words to get yourself off the hook. To truly receive absolution is to acknowledge the impact to the other person.

It's not enough to say, "I'm sorry I cheated on you," but to say, "I cheated on you even though I knew it was going to hurt you. For the hurt I caused to you and our relationship, I am sorry."

When you're able to look at a situation without being triggered, you're able to see the pieces of your life's spider web as they fit together with the web of the other person.

Asking for Guidance

I'm often reminded that the process of healing doesn't happen when and how I want. Complete healing rarely happens all at once. Every situation has layers, and they unfold on their own timeline, like a spiral on a shell.

Many evenings before going to sleep, I express gratitude for my day and ask Spirit to show me what's next. Sometimes, guidance comes in a dream. Oher times, in a thought as I'm waking or as I journal. Every time I've asked for guidance, I have received it. Spirit always brings the exact thing I need. Even when it feels hard and the old emotions are challenging, I know it is right.

Making Things Right

How do you create something better for the children around you while you heal and find your voice? How do you make amends to your adult children or family members who experienced you living through your shadows and silencing?

Be open. Be willing to see your side of a situation. See your family's cauldron of energy and how old rules may have created an unwanted pattern. Look more deeply at the bigger picture of those who harmed you. Be willing to have a conversation, make amends, and listen without needing to say a word or justify anything.

This begins the healing process.

ACCEPTANCE IS A RADICAL ACT

Forgiveness and clearing the energy between you doesn't require their participation or their physical presence. They may never participate. You can stop waiting.

Forgiveness means looking at a situation from all sides to find the lesson and come to a neutral place.

Forgiveness is something you do for yourself. You don't have to agree on what happened. You don't have to suddenly trust the other person.

Forgiveness is something you do for yourself.

Accept the situation for what it was and find peace with it. Acceptance is an active and radical act. However, acceptance doesn't mean agreement.

What if the lessons were to love yourself more, to release yourself from the negative messages from someone else's pain, and break the cycle of silence from past generations?

You know you're complete with a situation when you're no longer triggered. You have nothing more to heal. What power to both look back and also create forward momentum at the same time.

Clear the energy around your heart from a deep place of reverence.

CLEARING THE COBWEBS

"Ho'oponopono" is a beautiful Hawaiian poem of healing:

> I'm sorry.
> Please forgive me.
> I love you.
> Thank you.

"I'm sorry" is where you look at all aspects of the situation with another. The other may be another person, or it may be an aspect of yourself that's come up through reading this book. It may even be God. You take full responsibility for your part.

"Please forgive me" is where you shift the energy from focusing on the hurtful thoughts or behaviors to releasing and clearing. You make things right.

"I love you" is where you heal the rift. You focus on the energy of love from your heart.

"Thank you" is where you step into acceptance for what is. You see the lesson, whether it is finding your voice or seeing a true aspect of yourself.

Say this poem out loud or quietly to yourself, over and over, until you feel the energy shift. It can bring you to a beautiful space of neutrality.

This process communicates with your higher self to clear the energies at levels well beyond the physical.

A HEALING HIKE

During my travels, I did this on an eleven-mile hike to a hot spring. When a situation or a person would come to my mind, I repeated the poem over and over, with the intent to go beyond the ego and connect our higher selves.

At first, my focus was on the hurt from the other person. Once I saw that and cleared it, I opened the space to see my part. Repeating this poem cleared the energy from both sides.

Once I felt complete, I gave myself some space to breathe, then asked for the next person. I was surprised at who came into my mind's eye. I asked, listened, and heard.

This is a beautiful way to clear old energies, while also connecting in nature. If you're not able to physically get outside, nature for you may be a peaceful picture that you gaze into while doing this.

Your Invitation: Use this poem and process with Ho'oponopono to clear the energy between you and another. Transcend the old idea of forgiveness and engage your higher selves. Use it to heal your relationship with younger aspects of yourself, such as clearing layers of anger about internalizing what wasn't yours, for judgment toward yourself, or self-blame for tolerating an unhealthy relationship or situation.

CHAPTER 7
REMEMBERING JOY

"I come into the peace of wild things who do not tax
their lives with forethought of grief... For a time
I rest in the grace of the world, and am free."
~ Wendell Berry

TRUST

Trust comes back in pieces and waves. The truth is you never lost it. You don't need to find it, you only need to remember and feel safe enough to allow.

Trust requires safety. If you don't feel safe, you will feel challenged with knowing what and who to trust. Safety and trust go hand-in-hand.

When you trust, you remember who you are beneath the layers of rules and the paradigms that were instilled in you as a child, before you went into reaction mode, before you placed hard shells around yourself and your heart.

What if all the negative things you heard aren't true?

Consider that those people were speaking out of their own pain. Nothing is wrong with you. You are not broken.

You can break through the walls you've placed around yourself until you no longer listen to those old stories.

When you don't know how to process your own emotions, you project your feelings and emotions onto those around you. This is especially true when you're triggered. You might have a sub-conscious memory of your pain. You might see someone's light as a trigger of what you can't see in yourself.

People are triggered by being triggered. It puts them on edge, and on defense, because what are they supposed to do with their emotions?

A beautiful book entitled, *The Impersonal Life*, by Joseph S. Brenner is a mystical book that imparts messages of deep faith and the peace that comes through when we are in the world and not of it. Most actions aren't personal toward others, even when someone else is affected. People act and react out of their own pain, insecurity, or strength.

This doesn't mean that what people say or do doesn't affect you, but it relieves you of the never-ending thought bubble wondering what you did wrong.

THE GIFT OF GRACE

Think back to situations where you instinctively knew an answer to something and overrode it, only to realize down the road that you were right. Trusting your intuition can feel foreign at first, particularly if you grew up unsure about what or who to trust. Give yourself grace.

Trusting your intuition can feel foreign at first.

Grace is allowing yourself the time and space to explore. Think of a tree that has shed its leaves. Its roots still go deep within the earth. It may look like nothing is happening, but there's still movement in the quiet and stillness.

Grace is honoring the process of asking your higher self for guidance and then listening. You can't earn grace. It is an unearned gift and comes when you focus on the highest good.

This may feel odd at first, but what comes through is always what you need to hear. This is how you move beyond the silence of the old, where your energy used to be internalized. You move into a world where you honor silence as you honor yourself. Move beyond the chatter in your mind about who did and didn't do what to whom. This is healing

In your formative years, you may have had little room for mistakes. If perfection was an unspoken rule because you were tormented for not getting things right the first time, your expectation of how you need to show up in the world may have become misaligned.

It's time to let yourself off the hook from someone else's expectations.

Unraveling Right Now

Perfection doesn't exist. Perfection is an offshoot of fear. It's a trauma response. If you don't know how to begin and end, you were probably taught to be wide open or completely closed. When you feel like you're always in a bullseye, you may not feel safe to share yourself or what you've created.

Perfection doesn't exist.

You don't have to solve everything yesterday. You didn't get to this place overnight. Unraveling and unwinding yourself won't happen overnight either. It's okay to take a few deep breaths.

To see how your spiderweb is built takes time. Everything doesn't magically appear at the snap of your fingers just because you want it to. If everything came to you all at once, your head might feel like it's ready to explode. You're not meant to see it all right now.

As God reveals a piece of the puzzle, you process and integrate it. The next appears when it's ready. This is divine magic.

Grace allows you time to process and to walk through walls of resistance when they show up.

MAKING SPACE

This is why it's important to let go of trying to change anyone's mind except your own.

Grace is also allowing another person to have their feelings. You may make amends, and they still may not come around. The most important thing to do is to clean up your side of the tracks and move forward.

Communicate in an appropriate way. See people as they are, not as you want them to be. This may mean you have no place for them in your life moving forward. Rather than trying to hold on to someone who holds you back, let them go with love and compassion for their journey.

Your priorities are ultimately about making space within yourself with awareness, clearing old pieces of darkness, and taking ownership of what is yours.

STOP DRINKING THE KOOL-AID

You are not the old labels, the old hurts, the family dynamics, or the stories. You are divine. Embracing this is how you connect with what is real for you.

The stories you've been telling yourself and the uncleared energies are standing in the way of what you want to bring into your life.

The silencing is like an energetic hangover from your early years, played out through repeated patterns until you stop drinking the Kool-Aid.

Silencing is like an energetic
hangover from your early years.

MAKING ROOM

As you clear old, pent-up energy, you create more ease within your body, and you have fewer internal stressors. Studies show the benefits of healing modalities, including somatic healing, yoga, and breathwork. These practices help your nervous system to relax and clear your mind. My clients experience this through our one-on-one work together.

Colleen's father allowed for no compromise. She wasn't going to win. He gave out a feeling of "you don't deserve it." Her mother grew up in an alcoholic household where she couldn't speak up, so she didn't defend Colleen. As a result, Colleen had a deep lack of trust and the feeling she'd done something wrong.

The body has a finite amount of space. Healing makes room for the things you want to call into your life. Be willing to go there, despite what you were taught. Something beautiful will emerge on the other side, a little more every day.

Colleen created a new sense of normal for herself, which had been totally foreign to her—deeper trust of herself and her intuition. Then, she could live her ideal day in gratitude, take care of herself, and set strong boundaries.

ASKING A DIVINE QUESTION

Place your hand over your heart, close your eyes, and ask, "Who am I?" Sit and listen for an answer. Connect from a deep place of reverence for who you are.

You may not receive an answer right away, and that's okay. Connecting to universal wisdom is a maturation process. As you peel away the old stories, you open space within. You hone your intuition through practice, and sometimes, you'll receive an answer when you least expect it.

This is where trust and faith intersect. Have faith that you can do this. Trust that you will make the best possible decision for your highest good, and that you'll receive guidance when you ask from your heart.

WHAT BRINGS YOU JOY?

This question may feel challenging. Earlier in the book, we talked about the distinction between happiness and joy. This question asks you to look beyond external things that are fleeting and connect with that unshakable feeling deep within you, as you connect with your higher self.

CONNECTING WITH JOY

You may listen to this guided meditation by going to my YouTube channel, or read the following paragraphs.

Before you begin, have a pen and paper or a voice recorder available. Find a place that's free of distractions.

Get comfortable in a relaxed position, whether you're seated or lying down. Sit quietly with your eyes closed. Take a few slow, deep breaths, and relax.

The vision you connect with may be different than you expect. Your higher self will reveal what wants to be seen. This is where you take logic out of the process and allow what wants to arise to rise.

Picture a time where you felt complete joy, where you were totally uninhibited and fully free to be yourself. This may take a few moments, so be patient. Continue to slowly breathe, in and out while it forms in your mind's eye.

The first thing that comes to you is perfect. This is what wants to be seen. Feel into the energies of this joy and connect with it deeply in your heart. Allow it to flow through and all around you.

Now, connect with the details and give yourself a few moments between each question.

Where are you? How old are you? What's around you? What do you hear? Are there any smells? Do you taste anything? Is there a breeze? Are there any animals, plants, or trees? Are there other people? What are you doing?

Stay fully present with the feeling of where you are. Stay with this as long as you want and deeply connect with the experience.

Next, listen for a message. Imagine your higher self whispers into your ear. What message does it have for you? This message may only be one or two words, and that's perfect.

With your eyes still closed, imagine you hold out your hand and see a gift placed into it. What is this gift?

When you're ready, gently open your eyes and record what you experienced. How does this vision feel in your heart? How does it impact the stories you've told yourself or that others have told you?

Pay particular attention to how old you are in your image. The you at that age might want to be more deeply seen and heard.

This joy has always been inside you. You may have lost the connection because of life experiences. You can come back to this feeling of joy anytime you want because it's a part of you and nothing can take it away.

You can come back to this feeling of joy anytime.
Nothing can take it away.

This is powerful and enlightening, a moment that wants to be seen again. It may guide you as you reconnect with who you are.

My Experience with Joy

When I first did this meditation, I connected with my eighteen-month-old self. I was outside in my backyard, barefoot. I could see the individual blades of grass, and I could also see how they were connected.

My neighbor came to the back fence, a beautiful, young lady with an intellectual disability. We spoke via our hearts. Both of our language skills were limited. What an amazing and deep connection. Without that meditation the memory wouldn't have come to me, and the joy would have remained forgotten.

You have this power within you.

Your Invitation: Practice this meditation periodically. Different aspects of your life will come through. Even if you bring up the same situation, you'll see it from different perspectives and hear different messages.

Your strength comes from embodying your deep knowing, beyond your old stories.

CHAPTER 8
YOUR SOVEREIGN PATH FORWARD

"The only way to deal with an unfree world is to become so
absolutely free that your very existence is an act of rebellion."
~ Albert Camus

When you step forward to unwrap, understand, and
clear your internalized energies, you return to your
own deep knowing and trust. You connect with who
you are, the beautiful being beneath the layers. On this path,
you're also able to connect with profound joy, as well as safety
and trust within yourself, which are the basis of all things.

Turn off the noise of the external world and tune into the quiet
within. Even with guardrails and rules, what's right for your life
is a question only you and Spirit can answer.

---

*What's right for your life is a question
only you and Spirit can answer.*

This new framework begins with understanding the roots of
your stories and internalized energies, clearing them, and stepping onto a new path of connection and consciousness. You no

longer see yourself as separate, but you see the beauty in the connection of all things.

Listening to your intuition and your higher self is utterly crucial and underplayed in our culture.

Spirit is always here to guide you, if you choose to ask, listen, and connect. Spirit is also asking you to see yourself as it sees you.

THE JOURNEY OF THIS BOOK

Through reading this book, you've experienced a guided meditation to joy, exercises to deepen your understanding, and new tools to take you forward. You're on a path where you may never be the same again. This can be incredibly life affirming and powerful. As you move beyond the fear of the unknown, you reconnect with your divine self.

Through the contribution of my clients, my own history, and interviews, you've learned many of the ways silence impacts your life. I shared how I moved through my void, my metaphorical midlife crisis, and the beautiful things that came to me by saying yes to deeper levels of my healing journey.

Today, many feel like the caterpillar in the chrysalis. We're battling old paradigms, and generational appropriations of how we've been silenced. To find a new voice, we're asked to connect in new ways. Einstein was right.

You've learned how the centuries-old strategies of battle still play out today, not only in war but also in society, and how they directly affect our lives. This shift connects us more deeply from our heart. We use logic to support us, not drive us.

You've learned how your brainwaves, your subconscious, and the energies around you in your early years have a deep, lasting, and invisible impact into your adult life. You have also learned how the energies of your ancestors affect you and how to begin to clear those energies.

NO GOING BACK

As you move forward, the invitations in the chapters will help you connect with your spiderweb. You are under no obligation to maintain unhealthy relationships. Clear the energies, so you can be free.

You are under no obligation to
maintain unhealthy relationships.

The myths you've been taught are just that. You may look at them, smile, and say, "Thank you, but no." You're under no obligation to carry forward something that doesn't serve you.

Find the incredible beauty in seeing people and things for who and what they are, not as you expect to see them. Look at the world from a whole new perspective, one that removes the codependent chains from around your ankles and allows you to walk on solid ground.

You've learned the importance of giving a voice to yourself and no longer internalize your thoughts, feelings, and emotions.

You no longer need to remain silent and internalize your experiences. The old rules are just that. It's time to create a new paradigm for yourself—one of truth and healing.

Depending on where you are on your spiritual path, consciousness is waiting for you to connect with the essence that only knows love for you.

At first, you may not notice the changes within you. But when you reflect on how you were three months, six months, or even a year ago, you won't imagine ever going back. This is my wish for you.

THE BEAUTY OF THE PATH

What an incredible blessing to be rarely triggered by the past. When I do find myself triggered, I see it as an invitation to look more closely. The awareness that comes to me allows me to clear and clean up new layers of energy as well as layers of my cake. The gift of healing and the willingness to explore the deeper layers moves much more quickly when I don't resist.

The journey of healing lasts a lifetime, and beyond. It comes in waves that become gentler over time. Spirit no longer has to sneak in the window with a 2x4. There is always more to learn, and the more I learn, the more I realize how much more there is to learn about the deeper meanings of our interconnectedness.

I see the beauty of the path. I no longer see my experiences as the world conspiring against me, but rather as Spirit conspiring for me. Spirit has always been cheering for us all.

I'm defining a path co-created with Spirit. I dream about what the future holds. It feels safe to dream. I see the voids as spaces to play and wonder.

It's an honor and privilege to be a guide to help people purify their timelines and step more deeply into the truth of who they are. Many who find their way to me have done everything within their power to figure out what's in their way and were nearly ready to give up.

Healing and life aren't always logical, yet the pieces often reveal themselves in the most logical way.

I speak my truth from a place of love with tremendous joy in my heart.

A Poem for Trust

The following is a poem you may use to guide you through your days, perhaps as a promise to yourself.

Dear Trust,

Just for today, I am a fierce warrior for truth.
Just for today, I stand in my power and lead with love.
Just for today, I release others to their paths.
Just for today, I am connected with the Universe and receive with ease and grace.
Just for today, I take risks that result in my empowerment.
Just for today, I recognize and honor my specialness.
Just for today, I release and lift all fears of following my heart.
Just for today, I am fueled to carry through to create a happy life for myself.
Just for today, I am unabashedly me.
Just for today, I shine.

Join Us

Your invitation: Connect with me and join us in a world of like-minded people who are also on this path of healing. Together, we learn from each other, without judgment.

Connect with me via my website, The Way of the Diamond Warrior. www.wayofthediamondwarrior.com

Take back your power.

Learn powerful tools and techniques to
turn off the noise of the outside world.

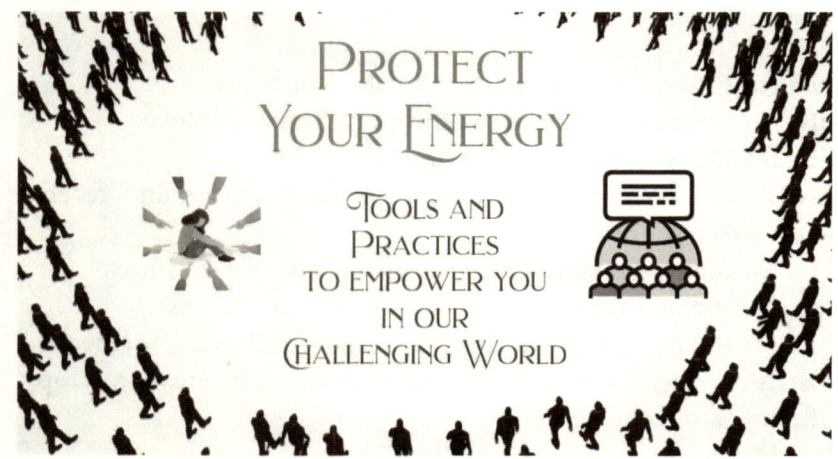

SCAN ME

Go to:
wayofthediamondwarrior.com/PYE

References & Resources

THE SCIENCE & DATA
CONNECTING THE DOTS

McAuliffe, Stephanie B., *The Message in the Bottle: Finding Hope and Peace Amidst the Chaos of Living with an Alcoholic.* May 2018

Way of the Diamond Warrior Website:
www.wayofthediamondwarrior.com

Montgomery Ph.D., John. "Survival Mode and Evolutionary Mismatch." *Psychology Today.* December 6, 2012. https://www.psychologytoday. com/us/blog/the-embodied-mind/201212/ survival-mode-and-evolutionary-mismatch

Knott-Dawson, ShaRhonda. "The Suffragettes Were Not Allies to Black Women, They Were Racist." *Education Post.* August 14, 2019. https://educationpost.org/the-suffragettes-were-not-allies-to-black-women-they-were-racist/

Fields-White, Monee. "The Root: How Racism Tainted Women's Suffrage." NPR.org. March 25, 2011.

https://www.npr.org/2011/03/25/134849480/
the-root-how-racism-tainted-womens-suffrage

"What Does Children Should Be Seen and Not Heard Mean?"
writingexplained.org.
https://writingexplained.org/idiom-dictionary/
children-should-be-seen-and-not-heard

Sinrich, Jenn. "4 Signs Your Toddler May Be Stressed."
November 19, 2021
https://www.whattoexpect.com/wom/baby/0204/
babies-sense-when-moms-are-stressed-out--which-stresses-out-
the-babies-too.aspx

Hewitt, John. "Scientists prove that fears and
memories can be inherited via sperm." December 4, 2013
https://www.extremetech.com/extreme/171990-scientists-
prove-that-fears-and-memories-can-be-inherited-via-sperm

University of Michigan Health System. "Learning the
smell of fear: Mothers teach babies their own fears via odor,
animal study shows." ScienceDaily. July 28, 2014.
https://www.sciencedaily.com/
releases/2014/07/140728153634.htm

Brainworks. "What are Brainwaves?"
https://brainworksneurotherapy.com/what-are-brainwaves

Gachot, Amanda. "Understanding the brainwaves of your children."
https://upallhours.com/article/
understanding-the-brainwaves-of-your-children

NeuroHealth. "Definition of Brainwave Frequencies."
https://nhahealth.com/brainwaves-the-language/

Teach Me Anatomy. "Development of the
Central Nervous System."
https://teachmeanatomy.info/the-basics/embryology/
central-nervous-system/

McLaughlin, Katie A. PhD; Sheridan, Margaret A. PhD;
Alves, Sonia BA; Mendes, Wendy Berry PhD.

"Child Maltreatment and Autonomic Nervous System
Reactivity: Identifying Dysregulated Stress Reactivity Patterns
using the Biopsychosocial Model of Challenge and Threat."
US National Library of Medicine. September 1, 2015
https://www.ncbi.nlm.nih.gov/pmc/articles/PMC4163065/

Waters, Sara F.; West, Tessa V.; Mendes, Wendy Berry. "Stress
Contagion: Physiological Covariation Between Mothers and
Infants." Sage Journals. January 30, 2014
https://journals.sagepub.com/doi/abs/10.1177/0956797613518352

"Somatic Therapy." Psychology Today.
https://www.psychologytoday.com/us/therapy-types/somatic-therapy

Dientsman, Allison Michelle. "Yoga Poses for Your Brain and
Nervous System." Goodnet. October 17, 2020
https://www.goodnet.org/articles/
yoga-poses-for-your-brain-nervous-system

HeartMath Institute.
https://www.heartmath.org/

Villazon, Luis. "What actually happens when a caterpillar
becomes a butterfly? Is it a Pokémon situation or more of a
Cronenberg thing?" Science Focus.
https://www.sciencefocus.com/nature/what-actually-happens-
when-a-caterpillar-becomes-a-butterfly-is-it-a-pokemon-
situation-or-more-of-a-cronenberg-thing/

STEPHANIE B. McAULIFFE

Jabr, Ferris. "How Does a Caterpillar Turn into a Butterfly?" *Scientific American.* August 10, 2012
https://www.scientificamerican.com/article/
caterpillar-butterfly-metamorphosis-explainer/

Weiss MD, Brian L. *Many Lives, Many Masters*, 1988

Brenner, Joseph S., *The Impersonal Life*, 1914

Acknowledgments

I am eternally grateful to my mother and father for saying yes and stepping into the unknown. We chose this journey together, and your love and support have taught me many things.

To all of the souls I crossed paths with, to see and be seen. In your way, you are each a catalyst and a mirror for this soul's journey.

To the many coaches and healers, who through your unique gifts, helped to guide me back to the trust within myself and the sovereignty of my soul.

There are far too many to list, however, our work cracked me wide open.

Your groups were a safe nest for this bird to be fed and to grow. Examples of the beauty of creating a safe place to explore.

Examples of what it is to be a witness for each other in our vulnerability as we step into the next level of ourselves.

You led me on uncharted paths, where I connected back into the mystical realm I'd lost touch with in my early years.

May I aspire to have the same impact on others as you've had on me.

To Tricia Brouk. Being on your stage is an honor, and being a part of your communities is a true gift.

To my clients and students who help me see the perfection in us all.

Last but certainly not least, a huge thank you to the team who help make this book a reality. To Lana McAra, my dear friend and colleague, for your editing expertise. To the team at JETLAUNCH for the design and layout of the cover and text, and all things publishing.

ABOUT THE AUTHOR

Stephanie B. McAuliffe is the Founder and CEO of The Way of the Diamond Warrior. She leads this revolution to shed the old rules and vestiges that no longer serve you, to step into your power and your truth, and to embody the peace that's your birthright.

Stephanie speaks extensively about how to find our voice and step into our true selves. As a teacher, personal transformation guide and energy healer, her passion is to help humanity heal trauma through boundaries. She focuses on our human condition and what it means to truly heal and break inter-generational cycles. She deeply understands the impact of trauma held within the body and the importance to our vitality to clear and heal it.

Stephanie's clients span the world, and she finds great joy in seeing them transform before her eyes, always seeing the light and perfection in who they truly are. She's helped thousands find their sense of self and unravel their patterns.

She's the author of the international best-selling book, *The Message in the Bottle: Finding Hope and Peace Amidst the Chaos of Living with an Alcoholic.*

Connect with Stephanie at: www.wayofthediamondwarrior.com

www.ingramcontent.com/pod-product-compliance
Lightning Source LLC
Chambersburg PA
CBHW031428120626
46545CB00006B/2318